Success Explosion In Every Aspect of Your Life!

Rob Vivian

ISBN: 978-1-77374-028-7 (print)
ISBN: 978-1-77374-029-4 (eBook)

Content Editing by Michelle Balfour, Your Novel Experience
www.yournovelexperience.com

Cover design by Ana Chabrand, Chabrand Design House,
www.anachabrand.com
Typeset in *Palatino* with *Bernard* display at SpicaBookDesign,
www.spicabookdesign.com

Printed in Canada

Acknowledgements

Being in a position to write several books would not be possible without the help of all the important people in my life. It really is difficult to name everyone, as there have been many.

My parents, Fran and Norm, have had the greatest influence on my life, teaching me a wide range of life skills. My wife, Coleen, is the person who keeps me grounded, as my mind sometimes gets away from me.

My children, Josh and Corissa, are really awesome, and very helpful around the company. My siblings Norma, Randy, Rick, and Eric always have my back, which is comforting to know.

I have a large sphere of friends who are always helpful and supportive. Our coaching clients are amazing in every way; I can't thank them enough.

Last, but certainly not least, I thank God for all my blessings: I certainly have more than I deserve!

Other Books by the Author

The Grass is Greener on This Side of the Fence

The Realtor's Magic Formula

Contents

"The people who are crazy enough to think that they can change the world are the ones who do."

Steve Jobs

For Starters

My attempt here is to teach the required principles to produce a bona fide *Success Explosion* in all the aspects of a person's life. This book is in no way suggesting that a *Success Explosion* is directly connected to money, or at least not solely focussed on monetary gain.

Of course, it is true that the implementation of the attributes contained in these pages would result in a more favourable financial position; however, the characteristics discussed are far wider-reaching than a more comfortable bank account.

My motive is on a much larger scale: to have an effect in every aspect of a reader's life, be it spiritual, physical, mental, familial, social, or yes, of course, financial. The *Success* principles discussed in this book will be just as beneficial to a person's health or relationships as they would be to their financial success.

It's my goal to, in some small way, play a part in the improvement of your overall well-being. It would be a mistake to apply these principles to only one area of your life when all could be benefited.

I'm very passionate about the content contained in this book; I hope that you find the material helpful, and can in turn apply each principle to benefit every level of your being. ENJOY!

Success Explosion
In Every Aspect
of Your Life!

One

Get Over Things Quickly

The first, and most important, of all the characteristics required for a person to have a *Success Explosion* in all the aspects of their lives is the rare ability to *get over things quickly*. Possessing this essential ability to overcome situations, obstacles, and setbacks is a lot more uncommon than most people realize. Everyone says they can "get over it" quickly; however, the truth is that few truly have this skill.

In life, things happen, be it business or personal: it's a part of the growth process. You can't have success in any area of your life without a few setbacks. In fact, a "few" setbacks would be uncommon; usually, numerous challenges are encountered before a breakthrough is achieved.

As an example, if you are striving to reach peak physical condition, it would be unreasonable to expect perfection from yourself. Could you achieve your goal of that perfect body? To, some day in the future, look in the mirror with awe at what you have created? Of course you can. However, to think that you would earn that result without some stumbles along the way would be a little unrealistic.

The process of transforming your physical appearance would take time. Along the way, there will be that banquet, where the only honest way you can describe the amount of food you ingest is as an abuse to your physical being. And there will be those times where you skip your daily workouts for a couple weeks, or don't put in your all when you're feeling dejected or under the weather.

These setbacks are to be expected, and calculated into the overall process. Nobody is perfect, and I would highly recommend that you stop pretending that you are. Things will happen; accept the mistake and get back on the right path. In this example, the one leading to a better, healthier body.

People do not like to admit that they hold themselves to a perfect scale, and yet most still do so. Think about the person who, for whatever good reason, is on a quest for a better and healthier body. As soon as they have their first obstacle—maybe a week or so of lazing on the couch eating junk food—they think, "You know what? I can't do this." And there goes that dream of the perfect, healthy body, which probably would add years of quality to their life.

If you were to ask this individual, "Do you expect perfection from yourself?" they would respond with an emphatic "no." However, the evidence points to the opposite.

Perhaps this same person hired a personal trainer to assist when they couldn't do it on their own. If they asked the trainer, "If I stumble along the way, is that going to be a problem?" I can assure you that the trainer would smile, or maybe even laugh out loud. The answer would clearly be: "Trust me; you will drop the ball a lot. As a matter of fact, you will think about quitting along the way—that I can guarantee you." Their trainer would not let them give up on themselves; because even when they try, the trainer will have already built error into their plan.

I can guarantee you that, no matter what path you are on in life or whatever goals and dreams you may have in your sights, there will be obstacles along the way. It can't go any other way: they are a part of the process.

If you can't have success without them, then the trick would obviously be to *get over them* as quickly as possible, and keep moving in the direction of your desired goal.

I, of course, cannot predict how many challenges you will encounter on the path to your *Success Explosion*. But for fun, let's say that on your way to that goal of the perfect body, five challenges lie in your path. Obviously, the longer you agonize over them, the further you push away from your desired result.

3

Every coin has two sides, so that also means that the faster you accept both responsibility and the fact that you are human, the faster you can get back on track and keep moving toward your ultimate goal. At the end of the day, dwelling on things will only be a hindrance for you, in every area of your life.

Therefore, of all the characteristics required to experience a *Success Explosion* in every area of your life, the ability to *get over things quickly* is by far the most valuable. In fact, the rest of the attributes all function on the assumption that you have mastered this first and most important trait.

There are a number of tricks that, if you master them, will grant you the knowledge necessary to count this ability to *get over things quickly* as something that is on your conquered list.

Keep Things in Perspective

Many people make things out to be worse than they really are; they build them up into something big in their head, and make too much out of a particular scenario. This habit is the opposite of getting over things quickly; this is, in fact, making a mountain out of a mole hill.

Let's go back for a moment to the person that is endeavouring to recreate their physical condition. Let's say they do have that couch potato week. If they can't *keep things in perspective,* there is a really good chance that they are going to give up on their dream.

Compare that to a person that does, in fact, have the ability to *keep things in perspective.* They may say, "Well, I screwed up this week; however, it's just a small lapse. Tomorrow, we'll be back in the saddle."

In life, serious things will occasionally come your way; there really isn't any way around that. However, most days your obstacles will be in the minor category.

Let's say that something pops up that, on a scale of one to ten, is a six. Okay, a six is something significant; it's not a ten, but it's also not a one. A six is up there on the list. However, let's treat it as it is: a six. Let's *keep it in perspective.*

Most people can't seem to *get over things quickly;* they miss the importance of *keeping it in perspective.* Yes, something that is a six on a scale of one to ten is probably something that's going to require some attention; however, if we can't *keep it in perspective* and we can't seem to *get over it quickly,* this six is soon going to become a ten.

Obviously, if everything that we encounter escalates to a ten, we are going to have a problem accomplishing any-thing—never mind the lofty goals we have set that will impact all the aspects of our lives.

Look for Solutions

If we can accept the fact that setbacks will happen, then we can also agree with the fact that we should *keep them in perspective.* Which means that when problems occur, we should automatically *look for solutions.*

Let's take a look at a business world example. Perhaps a client expresses frustration that you haven't been keeping in touch at the level that they expected. No business person would particularly enjoy that conversation; however, it is best to *keep it in perspective* and *look for a solution.*

Perhaps, after considering the facts, you conclude that the client was correct in their assessment. "I have been a little busy lately; from now on, I will implement a system of updating all clients every Monday after lunch."

To overreact to the client's venting would be demonstrating that you are not *keeping it in perspective,* and maybe prove that you haven't quite conquered the concept of *getting over things quickly.* Be a solution-driven person, not a person driven to dwell on matters.

Every Day is a New Day

"Every day is a new day" is an overused cliché, for sure; however, that doesn't mean that it's not true. On our path of life, things pop up along the way. It's not good to carry them into the next day, because *every day is a new day.*

Obviously, some things will be transferred from day-to-day; however, if possible, let's deal with it today. We'll put it to bed and start a new day fresh. Tell yourself, "It happened. I'm going to *keep it in perspective:* I'm going to *get over it quickly* and move along; dwelling on it will not lead to a positive outcome."

It's important that we don't start days with carry-over problems from yesterday. It's possible that today could hold a few challenges of its own; best to start every day fresh.

Leave yesterday's challenges in yesterday; yesterday is gone. Today is today, and it's important that we don't start in the hole. If we do, things will begin to compound, and before you know it, we are going to be the person that continually says, "When it rains, it pours."

Every day is new day. Let's leave yesterday's challenges in yesterday, and give today the attention it deserves.

Forgive

When we think about forgiving, we most often think about forgiving others for the transgressions committed against us. However, this point is bigger than that: much bigger. Although it's true that we must *forgive* others, it's equally, if not more important, that we possess the ability to *forgive* ourselves.

If we commit an act or thought that, within ourselves, we know was incorrect, it's imperative that we have the ability to acknowledge the indiscretion. We must make restitution in our own minds, *forgive* ourselves, and move along. *Get over things quickly.*

We need to learn to *forgive* and forget. I know—easier said than done. However, it is still necessary. Forgiving others isn't really for their benefit: it's for yours. Once you have forgiven them, you have the ability to move along. In doing so, you would also have given them the necessary piece to allow themselves to move past whatever dilemma has come between the two of you.

In many cases, once you *forgive* someone, they continue to dwell on the hurt and drama—in some cases for the rest of their lives. That's truly unfortunate; however, be clear that it's on them. If they choose to waste valuable time, if they choose to dwell on past hurts, there's nothing you can do about it. You forgave them: you released yourself from the burden and continued the process of enjoying your awesome life.

We think that, when we *forgive* someone, we do them a favour. And I guess there is some credence to that thought. However, the benefit of forgiving someone is the benefit that you receive.

When forgiving others, the contribution you receive far outweighs what you are giving away. You may think that you are punishing others by not forgiving them, but in fact, you are punishing yourself.

This chapter is about *getting over things quickly*. Don't dwell: *forgive* and move along. Life is truly short, so don't take something trivial to your grave.

Don't Live Under a Cloud

If you can't master how to *get over things quickly,* your life will be lived as if you are living under a cloud: walking around every day with a bit of a chill, not feeling the warm sun on your face.

I think you will agree that living your life as if every day is a cloudy one wouldn't be much fun. But let's be clear: if you are holding onto something, something that you can't seem to let go of, you are, in fact, choosing the "cloudy day" option. I would recommend that you immediately let go of whatever you are holding on to, and enjoy a sunny day.

Enjoy Time Off

As a result of getting out from under those cloudy days and getting over obstacles quickly, you have an opportunity to enjoy the time off that comes your way. I am totally, one hundred percent, against the "workaholic" mindset, and am vehemently opposed to the concept of "work hard now, enjoy life later." "Later" is not assured: now is what you have. You can, in fact, have your cake and eat it too.

So work hard on work days with a clear conscience, and enjoy the sunny days manifested by your ability to *get over things quickly.* In return, you will also capture another benefit: *enjoying time off.*

I mentioned earlier that if you are a person that holds onto things, every day will appear as if it's cloudy. Unfortunately, that will also translate into your time off: your personal time.

You have probably heard the saying, "the best of both worlds." Time is valuable. Be a person that *gets over things quickly,* so that you can enjoy both worlds of your productive work time and your valuable personal time with friends and family.

In a Nutshell

The principles required to have a bona fide *Success Explosion* are driven by the ability to *get over things quickly.* When setbacks happen in life—and they will—don't dwell; make the necessary adjustments and move along.

The principles in the following chapters hinge on your ability to master this particular principle. Holding onto things will literally be like running through water throughout your life. Do yourself a favour and let those things go: life is much better that way.

Helpful Exercise

Having a *Success Explosion* will require that you currently possess the ability to *get over things quickly*. You must acquire the skill to move past things when they do not align with your worthwhile life goals.

Completing the follow exercise will assist your brain in the discovery of items that are currently hindering your forward progress.

List three things that you, and everyone who loves you, know that you must move past:

Item #1

Item #2

Item #3

These items could come in the form of a relationship, a habit, or something that has happened to you in the past. The truth is, if you are aware of it, odds are that everyone around you is equally aware.

Admitting to yourself what you have known all along and writing it down is the first step to getting beyond each of those challenges.

"To heal a wound, you need to stop touching it."

Anonymous

Two

Live in a State of Gratitude

The topic of *gratitude* is the second chapter because it's the second most important of the traits necessary for a person to activate a bona fide *Success Explosion*.

That said, Chapter One, *Get Over Things Quickly,* is the most important attribute: all the others hinge on it. The following principles can't work if you can't figure out a way to move past situations as life brings them to you. So to be clear, the ability to *get over things quickly* is by far the most valuable of the required skills, by a long shot.

Living in a state of gratitude will require some work on your part if it does not come naturally to you. For whatever reason, for many people being *grateful* on a daily basis is second nature.

It's been said that we all come pre-wired, to a certain degree; you may see this if you have multiple children, whom you have raised with the exact same principles and values, that have still managed to turn out dramatically different.

Of course, as parents our job is to raise our children to be good people and law-abiding citizens. But if you are a parent, you know what I mean when I say that they come, to a certain extent, pre-wired. Some people are naturally *grateful*, while others: not so much. If naturally *grateful* is your position, that's amazing. If it's not, let's acquire the ability.

This book is about having a *Success Explosion* in every aspect of your life. Living daily in *a state of gratitude* will go a long way toward achieving that ultimate goal. We often hear the phrase, "they are a glass-half-full—or glass-half-empty—kind of person."

Glass-half-full people tend to be those that, on a daily basis, take the time to acknowledge the things in their lives that they are grateful for. Think about it as a life-style: you automatically *live in a state of gratitude*. When life's challenges come up, you are in a much better state to look at things in a positive manner: "glass half-full."

Let's pretend you are at work. It's 11:00am, and you have been up since 6:30am. Early in the morning, you are counting your blessings and *living in a state of gratitude*.

As your kids go off to school, you thank God for them. On your drive to work, you pass people at the bus stop waiting for their ride, and think, "I'm so thankful for the fact that I'm able to drive to work."

As you navigate your day, you notice little things that

make you realize that, although you might not be the richest person on Earth, overall things are pretty good.

Now, back to 11:00am. Your boss is having a bad day and taking it out on those under their jurisdiction, you included. Others will overreact: they will take it personally and allow their day to be thrown off: "glass half-empty."

You, on the other hand, are much more resilient; after all, you have had four and a half hours of grateful thinking on your side. Your spin on this common situation is, "Well, there is probably more going on here than I'm aware of. Maybe my boss has a personal issue that's troubling them, or maybe they are taking some heat from their superior and passing it along."

If you really think about it, that's the type of person you really want to be. Unfortunately, without the hours of grateful thinking leading up to this challenging situation, you would likely fall into the glass-half-empty crowd. Seeing that most people are glass-half-empty thinkers, you would at least have a lot of company.

Imagine the difference between these two co-workers arriving home for dinner. Their spouse asks, "Hey, how was your day?" The glass-half-empty thinker: "Unbelievable. My boss is insane. Truthfully, I don't know how much longer I can put up with this nonsense."

Now let's take a look at the glass-half-full thinker: "Hey,

how was your day?" "Great. My boss was in a bad mood, but there's probably something else going on; I'm just not aware of it."

Just as a side note, if a company needs to promote someone from within, which employee would be the likely candidate: the glass-half-full, or the glass-half-empty employee? Which mindset is more conducive to being promoted, in turn creating a much more significant career path? I think we would both agree that it is a rhetorical question.

Although this book, *Success Explosion*, isn't solely about money or careers, business success is a part of the package.

Most people, myself included, try to do the best they can to maximize their life. We try to be in a position to, when our time here is done, feel satisfied that we did our best, and remain confident that we left it all out there. If we live in a constant *state of gratitude*, we have a shot at this lifelong ambition.

There are other attributes and values that are also required for the ultimate goal of a *Success Explosion*. Unfortunately, if we can't find a way to train our brains to dwell in an ongoing grateful state, we will be stuck in a vacuum that is challenging to escape from.

If we go back to the workplace challenge, the employee that didn't spend their morning in a *state of gratitude* would really have no other choice but to overreact to the pressure coming from their boss, whether valid or invalid.

Obviously, the advancement opportunities for that employee would be limited. They could take their skills to another company; however, it's not their set of skills that hinders their advancement: it's their glass-half-empty attitude.

What You Deserve

I have a pretty busy seminar schedule, and it's common that I'm not the only presenter. Because of this, I hear the phrase, "You deserve it," a lot. I know, of course, that the speaker is just doing what they were hired to do: motivate and inspire people. However, I always wonder about that statement: "You deserve it."

I wonder if that is really true: do we deserve it? I believe that line of thinking creates a little bit of an entitlement mindset, which I, personally, think is a bit of a problem right now in our society.

To be perfectly honest, I believe quite the opposite: I think I have way more than I deserve. I have made a lot of mistakes in my life, many of which if I could go back and change, I would. But I can't, so as per the first chapter, *get over things quickly,* I move along.

I know this is going to sound a little anti-motivational, but I don't think we deserve anything; in fact, I think that if you were to honestly look at your life and how you have conducted yourself up until now, you would find it a frightening idea to receive what you really deserve. I would.

I find it a blessing that I don't receive what I deserve. Instead, I have received some amazing things in my life, which is quite the opposite.

I will say this, though, and this is a significant point: that although I don't think I deserve things just because Earth is my home, no one else on the planet deserves more. Truth is, maybe none of us deserve anything.

When I hear the phrase, "You deserve it," I always think, "That's actually not true: you don't have that entitlement." However, everything is available for you, for sure, and you should do your best to accomplish all you can while you are here.

We have a *Success Explosion* not because of what we deserve or are entitled to: we have a *Success Explosion* because of how we think and what we do. Living your life in a *state of gratitude* is an important piece of that puzzle.

In a Nutshell

Being *grateful* for what you have is a key ingredient to facilitate a bona fide *Success Explosion*. In no way am I implying that we should abandon our quest for personal growth and advancement; our commitment for improvement should remain steadfast. I'm just pointing out that, before we can think about advancing ourselves, we should first count our blessings.

The point of advancement is to improve our current position, not to create a whole new one. I am encouraging you to take stock of what you have: what do you possess right now that you are grateful for? What, through commitment and focus, can be improved upon?

I hope you do not seek to create someone that you are not. Start with being grateful for what you have, and build from there.

Helpful Exercise

Make a list of ten things that you are grateful for, and read it every morning. I would suggest that you leave your list on your night table, so that it greets you every day; if you put it in your drawer, you will likely forget to read it.

I am grateful for:

1) _____

2) _____

3) _____

4) _____

5) _____

6) _____

7 _____

8) _____

9) _____

10) _____

Some people wonder if they are too hard on themselves. If you have a challenge coming up with ten things that you are grateful for, then the answer would be yes. Lighten up and cut yourself some slack.

"Things turn out best for the people who make the best of the way things turn out."

John Wooden

Three

Set Worthwhile Goals

Setting goals in both your business and personal life isn't just important: it's paramount. On an importance level, I would place it up there with oxygen, which I think you would agree is pretty high on the list.

I'm sure this is not the first time that you have heard this advice: *set goals*. If you happen to be in the business world, it is commonplace conversation. Truth is, you probably hear it so often that you risk becoming numb to the dialogue; early on in my business career, I was certainly there.

I can vividly remember attending seminars, rallies, and conventions. The speaker would be talking about the importance of setting goals, and my mind would blank out, only to reconnect when we got to the "good part" of the talk. Although the speaker would move on to other helpful information, I spent a lot of my early career not realizing that *setting goals*, which I thought to be merely rudimentary advice, was in fact the critical information.

Sometimes we miss the simple things. Sometimes, we trade the simple for the complicated; we think that the more in-depth we go, the better or more important it will be. Nothing can be further from the truth.

If your life's path has not taken you down the business or entrepreneurship route, you may not hear as many conversations about setting goals; however, this is still a conversation that you are privy to on a regular basis.

And believe me when I tell you, if you are in sales of any kind, it is almost impossible to have a sales meeting without reference to the importance of setting goals; hence the numbness to this all-important topic. Let's take a look at some of the benefits of *setting worthwhile goals*.

Activates the Law of Attraction

I hear the term *law of attraction* a lot. When I ask business people about the *law of attraction,* they all claim to be aware of it, although they are not always sure how it works, or if it even applies to them.

What I find interesting is how some of the simplest things tend to confuse people: how, in many occasions, we tend to look right past the basic and go to what is perceived as the "advanced" material. The *law of attraction* works just as it sounds: on the same principle as a magnet.

Magnets attract metal. In your brain, you attract whatever you are thinking about most often. Hence the popular—and one hundred percent correct—statement, "You become what you think about."

In essence, you are a magnet, and whatever you focus on is metal: you attract that item. There are no grey areas here: if you are thinking about something, you are attracting it into your life.

The more you think about it, the more magnetic you are. If it's just a casual thought, then you are only slightly magnetic to that item. If, on the other hand, this particular item is an obsession, and it's the thing that you ponder all day every day, then of course you would be emanating a very powerful magnetic draw.

Some magnets are weak, with only enough power to pick up a coin. Others possess the strength to move a car in a scrap yard from one stack to another. The question you should be asking yourself is: what level of magnetism would you like toward your life's desires? Would you be okay with the level of magnetism that draws a coin, or would you prefer the ability to move a car?

I would say that the answer to this question is obvious; in fact, if you didn't answer, "Move the car," I would suggest that this book isn't going to be of much help to you.

If you can accept this *law of attraction*, you can then begin to understand why it's so important to *set worthwhile goals*. If you don't *set goals*, your brain will not have an item to make you magnetic toward.

It's unfortunate, really, how many people have a genuine desire to improve their position in life, to bolster all of their life's aspects, but do not bother to take this simple step. If they did, they would find it would dramatically move them away from a life plagued in mediocrity.

If you would like to be highly magnetic toward what you want in life, you need to first set those appropriate goals.

Write Them Down

In order for a goal to be valid, it must be written down. I often ask my clients if they have goals. "Yes, of course," is their immediate response. "Are they written down, or are they just in your head?" Sometimes they can show them to me; however, the more common response is, "Well, I didn't write them down, but they are clear in my mind."

I'm not saying that clear, detailed goals stored in your head are void of tangible benefit; after all, *you become what you think about*. If you are constantly thinking about the goals in your head, they will eventually become a reality in your life because of the absoluteness of that principle. However, writing them down is much better, and speeds up the process of achieving your worthwhile goal.

You might think, "Why do I need to expedite the process? After all, you teach patience, Rob." That's true: I certainly do promote patience. However, I do get a little concerned when people give up on their goals before they are able to achieve them.

If I were confident that everyone would remain focussed on the goals they have stored in their head, continually thinking about them and implementing them, then I would be fine. However, it's been my observation that most people with the ambition to make permanent change in their lives give up prior to the complete transformation.

If I were confident that everyone would see it through, I wouldn't have to promote *writing down* your goals as much as I do.

With the vast majority of people not possessing the ability to "stick with it," speeding up the process becomes critically important. If you are serious about moving your life to a new level, I would recommend you move your goals from your head onto paper.

There is something that you need to know with regard to writing your detailed goals down. According to neurologists, one hundred percent of what you write down is immediately transferred to the action part of your brain. This in turn activates the *law of attraction*, thus increasing your magnetism toward all your important goals.

We already know that if you think about something, you will attract that item; nobody disputes that. However, if you want to increase the magnetic draw, then transfer your goals from your head to paper; *write them down* and increase your magnetism.

As I previously mentioned, although you will eventually get there in the end, it's faster if you write your goals down. When you take a few minutes and put your dreams onto paper, there is a part of your brain that thinks, "Oh, we wrote this down; therefore, it must be important. No problem: why don't I send this over to the action part of the brain, so that we can draw this desired result to you."

I know that sounds a little rudimentary, but that is exactly what happens. *Writing down* your goals increases your magnetism and thus speeds up the process. This takes the possibility of giving up too early entirely out of the equation.

Gives You Drive

Clients are always asking me for tips and tricks to stay motivated: techniques to give them the necessary *drive* on a day-to-day basis.

There are many factors that might play into why someone would be residing in a complacent state. Lacking direction, they remain absent from the drive required to, on a daily basis, truly accomplish something extraordinary, be it business or personal.

When you write your goals down, you give that amazing brain inside your head a direction: a focus. It really doesn't matter which aspect of your life is requiring a *Success Explosion*; the process is exactly the same, whether your goal is finances (if your goal is entrepreneurial) or a desired weight (if your goal is in the physical realm). If you don't write down your goals, it really won't matter how much you want them on the inside.

It's like a ship setting out on a journey. The captain would first write everything down: he would "chart the course." Surely, if the voyage was from New York to England, the ship wouldn't set out and just sail around looking for England.

I know this example sounds ridiculous; however, that is exactly what most people do in pursuing their life goals. They only conjure them up in their head, and then get out and start moving toward them without first charting a course.

It's true that if a ship was to leave New York destined for England, upon leaving the harbour they would know which way to go. They might even end up in England. However, I think you would agree that they probably didn't take the most efficient route. A better idea would be to have spent the necessary time to plot the course and get things down on paper.

It's the same with your goals: take the time to write them down so that the path is clear. Then just sail down that path. Just as the engine of a ship will *drive* the vessel to England, your inner engine will *drive* you to your desired result.

In a Nutshell

If you don't take the time to think through what it is you really want, you will be busy going nowhere. "I may not know where I'm going, but I'm making great time."

Make decisions as to what you really want in life. Write them down, and begin the awesome journey to your worthwhile goals.

Unfortunately, most people spend their entire life and never achieve something that others would consider a small task. Some could spend years trying to lose 5 pounds. If weight loss is your target, decide upon your ideal weight, write it down, and start working toward it.

Your life has more important adventures than your ideal weight and physical appearance. However, if appearance has been your focus, you need to solve that item before moving on to other, more important, issues.

Void of setting goals, your life would resemble a sailboat without a rudder on a windy day: tossed to and fro at the wind's command. Set goals, write them down, and chart your course to your amazing future.

Helpful Exercise

All goals fall into one of three categories: somewhere to go, something to own, or something to do. List three things in each category, then put them in order of priority. Finally, add completion dates.

Places to go:

Location #1:

Date:

Location #2:

Date:

Location #3:

Date:

Things to own:

Item #1:

Date:

Item #2:

Date:

Item #3:

Date:

Things to do:

Item #1:

Date:

Item #2:

Date:

Item #3:

Date:

When we think about doing something, it tends to forever remain in the future. When we write it down and set a timeframe for completion, it tends to become something achieved.

"The greater danger for most of us lies not in setting our aim too high and falling short; but in setting our aim too low and achieving our mark."

Michelangelo

Four

Never Give Up

Once you have decided on what you really want, you must determine whether it is something that truly moves you at your core, or if it is merely something others think you should want.

This chapter is about *never giving up*: possessing the ability to stick with the dream. There is no doubt that challenges will come; it is part of the process. You can't have advancement without setbacks: they are married to each other. In order to have the required tenacity to stick it out, your aspirations must be deeply embedded in your soul; casual wants will not be strong enough to navigate the turbulent waters that lead to your desired result.

First, we need to decide what it is that we really, really, want: not just items that it would be nice to have. When setting goals and embarking on the voyage of accomplishment, our destination has to be something that "must" happen, not something that "would be nice if" it happened. For the things that would be merely nice to have, the desire for them is not going to be strong enough to overcome the challenges along the way.

Unfortunately, most people that set goals have this problem. Not enough time has been spent thinking through what it is that they really want. Therefore, the plan is usually abandoned at the first sign of adversity. The path to accomplishment is never without obstacles; mere wants have no chance of fulfillment.

On the other hand, it is also true that if you are chasing something that you want deep in your core, the challenges encountered along the way won't have a chance. The challenges will still happen, and they may disrupt your progress for a short period; however, in the big picture they will be conquered, because you will *never give up* on them.

As ever, I'm not talking about material gain. I'm talking about having a *Success Explosion* in all the aspects of your life. Will these principles still work to accumulate wealth and material things: houses, cars, boats, and money? Of course; it's just that life's bigger than that.

Should you be wealthy, with plenty of life's material pleasures? Sure—why not. However, that shouldn't be all you think about at the risk of ignoring life's more important features, such as spirituality, family, and health. If your financial and material desires are considered all-important at the expense of life's other aspects, somewhere along the line you got off-track in your values.

If money and material gain is all you are after, you can only experience one of two probable outcomes:

1)   Money and personal gain will always elude you

2)   You can make money, but you cannot accumulate wealth or security: you will simply be broke at a higher level.

Both of these realities are symptoms of a misled motive: some would use the term "shallow." If you relate to what I'm saying, it's probably not your fault: there is no shortage of books and training that preach "success at all cost," with the intent to simply gain as much as you can.

However, if you are searching for fulfillment in your life, you will not find it in material gain. Align the aspects of your life in the correct order, and things will flow to you.

I know it sounds strange, but if you would like a better financial position, then you can achieve that by placing money and material items in their proper order, such as:

1)   Spirituality

2)   Family

3)   Health

4)   Friends

5)   Financial position

You may not choose the same order as I did for the first aspects; however, your financial position (which includes material possessions) must be the least on your priority list.

I often get asked, "Are you saying, Rob, that if I improve the other aspects of my life, then my financial position will automatically improve?" Correct. Some would say that material things will flow to you once you have your priorities straight.

So, you must have your priorities in order to go after what you really want. Separate true desires from those things that would be "nice to have" and go after them with so much vigour that you will *never give up.*

Adversity Will Come

Without question, adversities will come your way. Since that's an absolute, I believe we should embrace it. Dealing with issues along the way creates many benefits.

Firstly, your sense of accomplishment will be greatly enhanced. If things came too easily, I'm not sure we would appreciate them at the level that we should.

Secondly, conquering life's little obstacles builds character. It's been said that what doesn't kill you, only makes you stronger.

There is really no doubt that setbacks are a part of the growth process; you can't have success without them.

In my coaching company, my clients know their numbers, and they know how many leads are required. They are also aware of how many losses are required. Armed with this information, they are more resilient to the knocks of business. When adversity crosses their path, they fully understand that these setbacks are both necessary and unavoidable. So rather than folding up like a cheap tent, they take it in stride. The challenges are chalked up as required, and they move forward; it's all a part of the process.

It's been said that the dance of success is three steps forward and two steps back. Personally, I don't think that this analogy is one hundred percent correct; however, the concept is absolutely accurate. You would be wise to factor in some amount of regression, whether it's two to every three or some other ratio. Either way, be sure that some loss of ground will occur.

What's interesting about this process is the dance of success is what should happen, not necessarily what is going to happen.

Let's say you have decided on your worthwhile goal. Right out of the gate you are making some progress: "three steps forward." All of a sudden, here comes some adversity: "two steps back." According to our dance, the next thing to occur is some more advancement: "three steps forward."

However, the thing that you must understand is that this is not necessarily what is going to happen. It's called "the dance of success" only when the route taken was successful, and your goal is achieved.

Seeing as most people do not achieve their goals, this would mean that the dance of success was not completed. So the question is: what would cause the dance to fail? What would cause this natural process to remain uncompleted?

If a person was to mentally buy into the negative momentum of the "two steps back," they would hinder the process of their next "three steps forward."

Let's just say that the "two steps back" took up two weeks of your time. If your mindset is strong, you would be able to handle these two weeks. The natural progression would be to then kick in some more effort for the next "three steps forward."

In a perfect world, that is how it's supposed to go. However, the common scenario is that too much mental drama becomes associated with the "two steps back," the inability to *keep things in perspective*. It is the result of overreacting to the *adversity that will come* when achieving a worthwhile goal.

When this happens, the two weeks allocated to the "two steps back" manifests into a much more serious situation. In most cases, this becomes a permanent obstruction to the natural flow of the next "three steps forward."

I wouldn't have any idea what percentage of people complete the dance of success in comparison to the number of those who halt their progress because they buy into the drama associated with the "two steps back." I would, however, feel confident to say that the vast majority of people can't seem to roll with the punches, manage their "two steps back," and quickly move to their next "three steps forward."

If there were a way to achieve your goals with nothing but smooth sailing, I would write a book on that. But seeing as I have not written that book, you can be assured that it doesn't work that way. *Adversity will come.* Achieving a worthwhile goal is a bit of a windy road, but there are many benefits to that fact, so keep moving in the right direction.

Never Settle

Given the number of seminars that I teach, I get really concerned when I hear people use words that make it abundantly clear that they are settling in life. Phrases like: "For me, this is good enough," or "I would be happy if I just had..."

I think there is a lot of pressure in our society for individuals to conform to what others believe is the "right" way to think.

For example, perhaps a young lady, who finds herself thirty years old, feels the pressure to conform to what others feel her life "should" be like at thirty. Maybe she settles for a mate just for the sake of conforming.

Perhaps a man feels that his body shape is not conducive to letting him look like the model on everything he buys. Maybe he starts to think, "So why bother? If I can't look like that person, I will just settle for what I look like."

I'm not saying that you shouldn't be content with who you are on every level. I'm saying you should never, ever, under any circumstances, settle for second best; if you do, you will come to regret it later in life.

It should be important to you to be the best person you can be on every level, be it father, mother, employee, husband, or wife. Whether it's in your physical, mental, or spiritual position, you should strive to be the best "you," yourself, can be. Not the "you" someone else wants you to be.

You must desire to improve yourself to become the "you" you want to be at every level of your being. You should never settle for less than your best. The words "This is good enough for me," should never escape your lips. It is better to not have something great than to never try and settle for less.

Anchors are Committed

The job of an anchor is to hold the boat in place. They have no secondary responsibility: hold the boat in place, and that's it.

Sometimes, the wind or current may be too strong for the anchor to do its job. Sometimes, it just can't seem to grab hold of the bottom long enough to hold the boat secure. However, you know it's functioning at its best capacity: everything that can be done to hold that boat in position is being done.

We would do well to have that type of determination in all our endeavours: the determination to do everything within our power to hold the various aspects of our lives in their ideal place.

Like an anchor, there will be times when, even with all your efforts, you just won't be able to hold yourself in your desired position. You must understand that no one is looking for better than your best, and so you shouldn't expect perfection from yourself, either. If you do, I'm sorry to say that you are going to often be disappointed. If you try your best and it still doesn't work out, you should accept the outcome and not become critical of yourself.

One of my passions is fishing. On some days, there is too much adversity for the anchor to do its job and hold the boat in the appropriate location. The winds or currents are too strong. I don't look at the anchor and think, "Come on, what kind of commitment was that?"

Obviously that would be ridiculous. I'm not going to run off to the fishing store to purchase a new anchor with "more commitment." I am one hundred percent confident that the anchor did its absolute best; if the adversity was too strong, then that's the way it is. Nothing more could be expected from my anchor.

Can you say the same about your commitment to the goals that you have set in each aspect of your life? Can you say that you did your very best, and the reason you fell short of your desired result was because the adversity was simply too strong?

If so, I would suggest you live with the result; if you did your very best and fell short, there is no shame in that. In fact, there is actually quite the opposite: you should be proud of your effort and accept the outcome.

Truth is, most people do not possess the unwavering commitment of an anchor; they give up way too easily, sacrificing their aspirations at the first sign of trouble. When an anchor feels a tug on the rope, this only causes it to dig in harder, grabbing for whatever it can find in an effort to keep the boat secured. We should do the same.

Sometimes, the pressure on the rope is too much for the anchor, and against all its efforts, the boat is left adrift. You will also find this in your life; I certainly have. Regardless of how hard we try, the pressure is just too strong, and adrift we go.

The key here is that, when we are occasionally at the mercy of life's winds and currents, we do our very best to hold ourselves in position. As you drift, your inner anchor will catch and secure itself once again, in turn giving you some control over life's little challenges.

There is no doubt that you will be adrift periodically in your life. You must have the commitment in your heart to grab hold and secure yourself. Applying the same attributes possessed by an anchor will simply leave you adrift a lot less.

This chapter is about *never giving up*. As I was writing this chapter and making the metaphorical connection to an anchor, I couldn't help but see the spiritual connection to "an anchor in your life."

Those That Never Gave Up

If you were to Google "those that never gave up," there would be an endless list of those that achieved greatness after an initial setback. I will mention just a few who prove that, under no circumstances, should you ever give up.

Walt Disney

Before he founded his international empire, Walt Disney was fired from his newspaper job for "having a lack of creativity." Can you imagine someone telling Walt Disney that he had no creativity? I think about all the classic Disney movies that I have enjoyed, not mention my time at Disney Land; I'm sure glad Walt didn't mentally buy into that comment!

Theodor Geisel

Theodor's first children's book, *And to Think I Saw it on Mulberry Street,* was refused an astonishing 27 times before it was published. Theodor went on to write a total of 47 children's books, selling an estimated 500 million copies. Clearly Theodor had this chapter figured out. Theodor Geisel is best known to the world as Dr. Seuss.

Elvis Presley

Elvis was told that he didn't possess the talent to make it in the music industry. I am so glad Elvis was not a quitter: karaoke at my house would be a lot less fun.

Colonel Sanders

Colonel Sanders' amazing chicken recipe was rejected an unbelievable 1,009 times before he had a taker. This chapter, *Never Give Up,* is a strength of mine. However, at 1,009 times rejected, Colonel Sanders is clearly better at it than me.

I'm just using these amazing people to make my point; I could use the next hundred pages to list names and scenarios. The truth is, almost every famous person would be on the list. It's actually very rare to become successful without adversity.

Those that ended up with success had an opportunity to pack it in early in their career, when their "anchor" was feeling some pressure. However, something deep inside was greater than the negative feedback they received, and their inner belief outweighed the setback.

The question you should be asking yourself is: do you have that type of inner belief in yourself? Are you resilient enough to hold your position, to stand firm in times of trial? Or are you going to pull back at the first sign of tension?

Thousands of other successful people possessed the mental fortitude to roll with life's punches. Rather than being knocked off-stride, they were somehow able to convert that negative information into motivation.

Just to be clear: this, too, will be necessary for your success.

In a Nutshell

Adversity will come: you can't have success without it. Everyone will experience challenges on their road to achieving their worthwhile cause.

The vast majority give up, and unfortunately never experience the fulfillment that they were capable of. A small group of people, however, push through: they use the negative situation as fuel to propel them to greatness. Be in that small group: *never give up!*

Helpful Exercise

We all have examples in our past where we simply gave up too easily. Perhaps those situations are still ongoing. Either way, we should be determined not to "settle" so easily.

List three things that you recently gave up on too easily, or items which are currently on the go that you are tempted to do so with. As you consider these items, it's important to understand that what you desire must be both morally and ethically appropriate.

Things that I should fight for:

Item Worth Fighting For #1: _____

_____

Item Worth Fighting For #2: _____

_____

Item Worth Fighting For #3: _____

_____

Again, this item must fall under the category of something moral: not harmful to another individual.

A worthwhile business goal or a desired weight would be good: coveting something that someone else possesses would be bad!

"Never give up on something that you can't go a day without thinking about."

Winston Churchill

Five
The Blessing of Contribution

Contribution is an interesting component in the success puzzle: it's not like the other moving parts, which are easy to quantify. If your athletic trainer sets out a workout or nutrition program, and you follow it to the "T", your results are relatively predictable.

Many of the pieces of the success puzzle are like that: do X and your results will be Y. However, *the blessing of contribution* is not one of them.

It's difficult to say you received this because you gave that. The amount you receive back is a bit challenging to allocate, whether it was from your financial or physical resources: maybe it was even your time that was your gift.

Those that are reaping the rewards of contribution in all aspects of their lives know that the more they give the more they get. When something amazing comes to them out of the blue, they can't really say, "This happened in response to me doing that." They just know that the more they give of their resources, the more that comes their way.

Every faith teaches this principle: give freely, and it comes back to you many times over. It's hard to know how many: double? Triple? Maybe ten times greater.

It's also difficult to track in which aspect of your life the blessing will be returned. For example, let's say you give sacrificially to a family member who was financially in need. Perhaps your generosity actually left you a little short, but you rationalized that their need was far greater than yours. Maybe it meant you couldn't go out for a nice dinner—a luxury—so that the receiver could have the basics in their fridge—a good call, really.

But just because your giving was financial doesn't mean that your reward will be financial. It just means that a reward is coming your way, perhaps to an alternative aspect in your life.

There is a catch to this principle, and it involves your heart: your motive must be pure. If you are being generous with the intent to bring good things in your direction, I'm sorry to tell you that it won't work. This principle hinges on a pure heart.

When I say a "pure heart," I mean pure in regard to the generous decision you have made. If this principle required an absolutely pure heart, we would all fall far short: way short.

In order for your heart to be pure, your motive must not be "to get." You must genuinely have a desire to help, not for the return or acknowledgement, but purely for the sake of assisting.

Every human being's responsibility is, among other things, to leave the planet a better place than we found it. If you give generously with the right motive, you activate a chain of events that attracts blessings in your direction.

Again, it's impossible to attribute this benefit to one action or another. It's not like you gave some money to someone in need and cheques start showing up in your mailbox. That type of thinking is misleading.

There are many areas of your life that you could receive a blessing in: perhaps the doctor gives you a better report than you were expecting to receive; maybe that near miss on the highway is exactly that: a near miss. Don't underestimate the principles at play on our planet and beyond.

Become a Mentor

Becoming a mentor is an excellent way to activate *the blessings of contribution*. At this point, you understand that, in order for the principle to be activated, you must possess the proper motive: your heart being in the right place is mandatory. If your motive is to give in order to get, I'm sorry to tell you that your expected return will go undelivered.

You can't view this principle as a vending machine: that you put your money in and out comes your selection. A vending machine is locked into a sequence, but this principle is not.

Those at my coaching company coach with the correct motive: if it wasn't, they wouldn't be coaches; at least, not for me. So they know from first-hand experience that being a mentor—the giving of their time, expertise, and resources—coupled with an honest desire to help people will bring amazing payback.

It's fascinating to watch our coaches at work: they are so eager to help other business people. As one of their prodigies rises to the top of their field, they receive an immense feeling of satisfaction that they played a small part in that process.

To coach for my company, there are really only two stipulations: first, they must be among those at the top of their field (the person being mentored must realize that their mentor has been or is currently where they desire to be). The second is what we are talking about right now: they must have a genuine desire to help others. Their motive cannot be for the prestige or an expected return.

Our program creates hundreds—perhaps thousands—of big hitters, and many enquire about being a coach. Only those that can line up with these criteria are considered.

What's amazing to watch is how the coach's life improves

on almost every level: to the point where, a year or so later, time management is their greatest challenge because of all the responsibilities that they have taken on. Although the payback doesn't always come in the form of financial benefit, it often does.

It's true that, because I own a real estate coaching company, my mind would automatically jump to business metaphors; however, I wish to emphasize that the material covered in this book is not solely for business people. In fact, it's not even tailored to the business world. I'm assuming that the vast majority of folks reading this book are not the entrepreneurs of the planet.

This principle is a universal one: give with the right heart, and receive back many times over. It just so happens that being a coach fits perfectly as an example.

Perhaps for you, your opportunity for *becoming a mentor* comes in the generous giving of your time to a young person that desperately needs that guidance and attention. Of course, all the same principles apply.

In addition, I should also mention that this principle is not bound by time. Therefore, if you are giving in order to "get," you will be very frustrated. The rewards of applying this concept are not something that you can put on your timetable. So if you give only to expect a result, then your days will be spent impatiently waiting to be rewarded. It is not a matter of, "Come on, I did my part";

if this is your intention, then your reward would not be forthcoming anyway.

However, if your true desire is to assist for the sake of helping someone else achieve something that is important to them, you can be certain to see some benefit, be it financial or personal.

If I'm describing you, then the fact that this principle is in no way connected to time should be just fine with you, since the thought of personal gain is absent from your mind.

I know all people like to say that they give for the right reasons; after all, it's difficult to say, "I'm only helping you because I'm looking for payback." Of course you would never say that out loud: no one would.

However, I encourage you to check your motive, deep down in your core. Most people do fall into this category; it doesn't make you a bad person, it just means that you have, somehow, obtained a bad quality. Work to replace it with an honest desire to better other people instead of constantly thinking about how you can improve your own position in life.

Hoarding is a Poverty Mindset

I can't think of any scenarios where hoarding would be beneficial to you. Whether it's things you collect or it's money, hoarding is void of any positive characteristics.

If you have any abundance of physical things, I'm sure there is someone not too far away that has a genuine need for that particular item.

You could, of course, look for an opportunity to sell your excess items, but this chapter is focussed on the benefits of contribution: giving for the sake of helping others who have found themselves in a time of need.

I love the fact that organizations call me to enquire if we, as a family, have any extra clothes or household items that we could donate to a worthy cause. Of course I say, "Yes," and put everything out on a designated morning for pick up.

We have a spot in our home where we collect excess items. As soon as they are picked up, we start a new collection so that we are ready for the next time an organization calls.

Occasionally, friends tell me, "You know, you could sell your extra things online. There are lots of apps for that; it's pretty easy." Of course I am aware of that; however, I think of *the blessing of contribution*. It is important to look for opportunities, even small ones, to make a gesture of kindness toward other people. There are many people out there who you do not know, but who live without while you live in excess.

The other day, I had a conversation with a client that turned into a large-scale coaching session. This particular client is an amazing person; however, we all make mistakes periodically, and somehow, someway, we get our brain focussed in the wrong direction.

To give you a bit of background, a few years ago this client was struggling in their business. It had gotten to the point that pursuing a new line of work wasn't just a consideration for them: the plans were already in motion.

It's always sad when you pursue something worthwhile, something you've poured all your energy into, and it just doesn't work out. Maybe you didn't quite know what to do at the time, or perhaps you didn't give the effort required; either way, at some point it's time to move along.

This was the exact scenario at play when I met this client: they were not really aware of what to do, and a little shy on the effort. Being unable to put in their "all" was hardly their fault: it is difficult to fully commit without a clear path (and thus Chapter 3: *Setting Worthwhile Goals*).

We met quite accidently, and they shared with me that this part of their career was about to change. When I enquired as to what they had been doing up to this point, it was no surprise to me that things had not gone according to plan.

Fortunately for this person, their desired path is what I do for a living. I suggested that they give it another ninety days, allowing time to make some adjustments and work on a plan that I would design for them.

They agreed whole-heartily; leaving the business definitely wasn't their first choice. After the ninety-day period, they were happy to report that their production had picked up, and to this day their business has been thriving.

More recently, what led to the wide-scale coaching session was them mentioning that everyone in their office was marvelling at their amazing turnaround over the past couple years: from one foot out of the business to top producer.

I suggested that they speak to their broker; I was happy to set up a seminar and explain to all my client's colleagues what exactly they had been doing. Then others, too, could experience the same benefits.

However, their initial response was, "I don't want them to know what I'm doing—then they will all do it."

You see, this client really is amazing; however, hoarding information to oneself is a negative quality. The object is to share what you have for the greater good.

I know that at first glance it may appear that you lose something when you share, but I can assure you that it's quite the opposite. It's contributing to others, with no stipulations for return, that makes you a magnet for success. Had we not had this particular conversation, it would have hurt this client over time.

Fortunately, this client is smart enough to have recognized their mental error right away. I did speak at their office to enlighten others to the path to being a successful person; many of them are now experiencing the rewards.

Interestingly, because of this meeting and my client's openness to share what they know, several unexpected opportunities have since opened up for them. That client is now a mentor to several others in the office, further allowing them to experience *the blessing of contribution*; quite the opposite to their original thought of hoarding that same information.

This story is a couple of years old at the writing of this book. Since then, that client's production has doubled. Is it all as a result of the contribution they freely gave to their colleagues? Maybe not, but it's certainly a piece of the puzzle.

Panellists

At my seminars, it's quite common for me to have several of our clients on stage with me for an interview. I like it, they like it, and the audience loves it. After all, they can only listen to me for so long. It's much more impactful to hear the message from someone who has taken the time and implemented the information I provide.

It's interesting for me to observe how intently the audience pays attention: their focus definitely increases. They are observing someone who is only slightly further down the path than they are: maybe just by a year or so. I can see in their eyes that they feel the gap between them and my panellist isn't as great as they thought it would be.

I know for certain that every client who has the opportunity to be with me on stage has the proper motive. They are acutely aware that their explanation of their mental advancements and what they have accomplished will have a huge influence on those present. Without being overly dramatic, their words may be life-changing for some.

Obviously, there is some notoriety to be gained within our circles with such an opportunity, so I must know whether their motive is an honest one: that they will share what they know with the pure intention of contributing information into someone else's life, with no interest or concern for something in return.

Although it's not uncommon for me to speak to only twenty or thirty people, it's also equally common for the audience to be upward of a thousand. When I have someone with me on stage in a larger meeting, that's a lot of contribution. In fact, part of my goal is to create outlets for them to contribute to others.

If you ever get the chance in your field, telling others from a stage exactly what you did and the impact those actions had on your life is an excellent opportunity to contribute. It would, in turn, activate this principle of *blessings of contribution*, assuming your motive is pure.

In a Nutshell

Contribution is a necessary component in the success puzzle. It can sometimes be hard to quantify, given that its rewards are neither bound by time nor restricted to the same vein as it was given.

The only stipulation is that you must be giving for the correct reasons. Many give only in order to receive, and will, of course, spend the rest of their days awaiting a return that is not forthcoming.

This principle of contribution isn't just a good idea for a *Success Explosion*. It's mandatory; just like gasoline isn't just a good idea for your engine: it's necessary to propel you forward.

Helpful Exercise

Contribution can take on many forms. You could possibly give of your time, or perhaps something material that you own. Maybe even a monetary gift.

I think most people like the idea of helping others, but in the busyness of life never get around to it. If we took the time to consider some possible opportunities and the ways to implement them, we could all easily experience the satisfaction and *blessings of contribution*.

Contribution opportunities:

Opportunity #1:

_____

Opportunity #2:

_____

Opportunity #3:

_____

When we contribute with the proper motive, we experience a reward far beyond what we contributed. If we contribute in order to activate the principle, I'm sorry: no cigar!

"Only those who have learned the power of sincere and selfless contribution experience life's deepest joy: true fulfillment."

Tony Robbins

Six

Positive Expectation

It's important that we live every day of our lives with the expectation that good things are on the horizon. We must believe that every new day brings a host of good things our way.

We have a bit of a ritual at my coaching company: every work day at 8:30am, I send a motivational message directly to my clients' cell phones. I always end every message by saying three times, "Something awesome is going to happen today." Most of my clients recite it with me. The purpose is simple: I want all of our clients to live every day with the *positive expectation* that good things will happen.

A really interesting benefit to this ritual is that, at 8:30am, many of our clients are on their way to school with their children. What could be better for young people than to hear a motivational message every day, informing them that they possess the power to do anything they want? To live every day with the absolute expectation that "something awesome is going to happen today"?

I can't really say how many of our clients listen to my daily message while driving their children to school: it's definitely in the hundreds. It is really encouraging for me to hear stories of children listening to my morning message.

One in particular comes to mind, which was very motivating for me. A client shared that each student in his 7-year-old's class was required to speak at the front of the room, on any topic they wanted, for two minutes. It's a great exercise to get the students out of their comfort zones. All the parents were present.

As you can imagine, a 7-year-old would most likely talk about their pet, a favourite sport, or maybe a recent vacation. But when our client's son addressed his class, he shared, in his nervous, 7-year-old voice, why awesome things should happen every day. How it was our thinking that got in the way and blocked those awesome things from finding their way to us.

Obviously, the other students were confused. The teacher was astonished, and all the parents were crying. As was I, when this story was shared with me. That's the result of several years of a message of hope landing in a young mind on a regular basis.

In some ways, the young mind is much more open, having not yet lived through the disappointments adults have endured. Nevertheless, we need to let go of the challenges of the past and move forward. We must live each and every day with the *positive expectation* that awesome things are coming our way.

Being a little less like an adult and a bit more childlike would be helpful. So let yourself go: drop your guard, and allow your imagination to run free.

You Become What You Think About

As an adult, you are quite aware that you become what you think about: your future is an echo of your thoughts today. This also means that everything you have today, in each of the aspects of your life, is a result of your past thoughts.

This concept, *you become what you think about,* really isn't open for debate: it's absolute. If we spend our days worrying about what could go wrong, we accidentally focus on the negative side of each and every situation. Thus, we will attract all the negative scenarios into our lives.

The fact that we don't want these items is inconsequential—"you become what you think about," not "you become what you are *supposed to* think about." The fact that you know better than to think of negative things has no bearing; if you are thinking those negative thoughts, then you are travelling in that direction.

The obvious solution is, of course, to be living with the *positive expectation* that awesome things are coming your way: that every day is a new day full of opportunity. This doesn't mean that life's natural flow of challenges won't come your way; of course they will. However, at least you won't be the one adding unnecessary stumbling blocks. When life does deliver a blow, you will be much more resilient to those natural setbacks.

You have a daily choice: to either live on the positive side of the ledger, knowing that "something awesome is going to happen today," or on the negative side. You often hear these people use the phrase, "Oh my gosh; when it rains, it pours."

Negative things will happen in your life, guaranteed; however, if you are not living with the *positive expectation* that things will go your way, you are probably believing that events are stacked against you. Unfortunately, this adds to the normal number of life's challenges. Hence, "When it rains, it pours."

Every day, a choice is required. I highly recommend you choose to live in a mindset of "Something awesome is going to happen today."

In order to experience a *Success Explosion,* you should fully reside in the expectation that awesome things will continually happen in all of the facets of your life. There are many reasons to do so, and I will share with you my thoughts and understanding so that they may assist you in the quest to master living in a state of *positive expectation.*

Living the Dream

This commonly tossed-around term, *living the dream,* has a lot more to it than we give it credit for at first glance.

Firstly, where does this term come from? Here in Canada, as well as the United States, families have been immigrating for hundreds of years. The story is always the same: to have a better opportunity for ourselves and our children.

Actually, it's usually for the children. In fact, most first-generation North Americans take on a lower-class occupation than they had in their homeland in order to create a better opportunity for their offspring.

It's quite common to hear someone say, "Back home, I was a physician (or pharmacist, lawyer, business owner); unfortunately, those credentials do not translate here." Therefore, they tend to work a far lower-paying job in order to get themselves assimilated into their new situation.

The reason someone may be willing to forgo a successful career and restart at the very bottom is for the bigger picture of what is best for their family: the opportunity of *living the dream.* I would think the thought of *living the dream* is on every newcomer's mind. It's really impressive to me to see how many people have chosen to take on this massive change and are *living the dream.*

Imagine a family that, as we speak, is in the process of immigrating to your community. They are excited about the opportunity to relocate and begin their journey of *living the dream.*

Let's pretend they meet you. Would they observe you and think, "That's exactly what I'm looking for—that's why I'm willing to make this huge, life-changing experience." Or would they observe you and think, "Hmm, I kind of thought that someone *living the dream* would be a lot more excited; a lot more positive"?

Sometimes the saying, "I can't see the forest for the trees" comes to mind. Here we are, living in a place that others dream about, and we spend our days bogged down with life's everyday challenges. We should instead be engaged in the pursuit of *living the dream,* spending our days with the belief that awesome things happen every day.

If you do reside in a land of opportunity, be it Canada, the United States of America, or another part of the free world, I hope you are *living the dream.* I hope every day you are squarely focussed on the bigger picture, and are not being dragged down by life's everyday issues.

Every single day, know that you wake up in the best place in the world, and attack that day in search of something awesome. Avoid being the person to say, "When it rains, it pours." Live the dream with an absolute, *positive expectation* that something awesome will happen today.

Overcome the Negative More Quickly

As per the first chapter, the ability to *get over things quickly* is by far the greatest factor as to whether or not you will experience a *Success Explosion*. When you are living your life in a state of *positive expectation*, it allows you to get over the bad or disappointing events more quickly. This is because you hold the absolute belief that awesome things will constantly appear in your life.

When you live in that mental state, it is a lot easier to *keep things in perspective*. There is no doubt that, periodically, life will deal us a big blow. On a scale of one to ten, this item will be a ten; something serious to have appeared in your life. If we are living in *positive expectation,* we will be a lot more resilient to these blows.

More commonly, our challenges are on the lighter side of the scale: maybe a five instead of a ten. Living in a state of *positive expectation* allows us to deal with our current life's setback as it is: a five. It better allows us to *keep things in perspective*.

I'm not saying that a problem that's a five isn't important; of course it is. A five is something that is going to require your attention, maybe at several levels. However, living in *positive expectation* will allow you to handle this challenge at the level it was introduced at: a five.

Considering that most people do not live in this acquired state of expectation, every challenge for them is a ten, whether those challenges are truly a ten or have been elevated from a five.

It goes without saying that if we are not living with the belief that good things are on the horizon, all of life's obstacles can easily escalate to a ten. However, when that's the case, it is difficult to *get over things quickly*. It becomes that much harder to put life's inevitable challenges in the rear-view mirror and keep moving forward to life's amazing adventures.

Count Your Blessings

Live with the belief that life will treat you well, and the *positive expectation* that adventure and abundance are around every corner. This state of mind also produces a few unexpected benefits.

One of these is that your brain desires to keep track of your progress as you travel through this awesome life of yours. It keeps track of both your accomplishments and your downfalls.

I would never suggest that when you live in a state of *positive expectation* that your life will be free of obstacles; of course it won't be. However, I am confident to say that when you are living your days in that constant state of expectation, your brain will automatically push those amazing experiences to the forefront and bury those that occupy the negative side. The negative experiences are still there: they are just not what run your life. Sadly, not as many people mentally live on this side of the equation.

When we dwell on the positive, we create an environment where we are constantly *counting our blessings*. When something happens that is not on the positive side of the ledger, something that we would like to get in the rear-view mirror as quickly as possible, it's a lot easier to handle when we can keep our blessings in mind. Our perspective becomes, "Well, this is a drag, for sure; but in comparison to all of the awesome things that have happened, it's not really that big of a deal."

Consider for a moment a person who has chosen not to live in a perpetual state of *positive expectation*. When life comes around with one of your unavoidable obstacles, this person won't have the luxury of weighing all of their blessings against this one unwanted visitor. I'm sure certain things have gone their way recently; however, due to their lack of living in *positive expectation*, their brain has not pushed all of these amazing items to the forefront.

Unfortunately for them, quite the opposite will be their reality. Their mind will automatically add this new setback to all the others that are not buried where they should be. And that is when the oft-repeated comment arises: "When it rains, it pours."

Everyone, of course, will experience the natural ebb and flow of life: the flow of things going their way and the ebb as things slightly roll back. You have a choice: to spend your time mentally focussed on the flow of life and burying the ebb, or being fixated on the ebb and thus burying the flow; it's your call.

It goes without saying that, seeing as we all experience both the positive and the negative, whatever we choose will be the reality we live in. If we choose to live with a positive perspective, we also pick up the side benefit of *counting our blessings,* of which there are many; it would be a shame not to acknowledge them on a daily basis.

You Don't Have to Go From Zero to Hero

We tend to live in an impatient society, one that has a need for instant gratification. Living in a state of *positive expectation* and believing that blessings are on the horizon allow us to be far more patient and understanding. The things that we want, and the position in life we aspire to, do not necessarily need to happen today: *We don't have to go from zero to hero.*

Things that are worthwhile often take time. Actually, they almost always take time: getting what we want instantaneously is quite rare. The trick would be to enjoy the process: to embrace the path from where we are to where we desire to be.

For those that do not possess the ability to be patient, this particular concept, that *we don't have to go from zero to hero,* is, unfortunately, their downfall. As a business coach, I see this almost on a daily basis: a client has a bad day or week, and they give up.

It's sad to see, really. However, we have to realize that if the client is absent of the attributes required for success—in this case, understanding that things will not go their way instantly—we as a company are limited in how we can help. I wish we could be patient for them, but unfortunately, that's not an option.

We can teach this principle, but the client is an adult who makes their own decisions; the responsibility clearly lies with them to understand that they *don't have to go from zero to hero.* Instead, better to sit back, be patient, and enjoy the ride.

Unfortunately, this occurrence isn't as rare as you might think; many people just can't seem to administer the required amount of patience. This results in premature frustration, which in turn leads to a logical outcome of failure.

Fortunately, an extremely large group of people can, in fact, recognize this incredibly important principle. They are able to accept the fact that what they really want doesn't necessarily have to happen today, and can enjoy the small victories along the way. "The journey is as much fun as the destination."

Many would say that the accomplishments earned along the way are more rewarding than the actual arrival. In fact, some have mentioned that the feeling upon arrival is somewhat anticlimactic. Do yourself a favour: be patient. *You don't have to go from zero to hero.* Take your time and enjoy the process: life is about the journey, not the destination.

Something Exciting Always Lies Ahead

Assuming you are patiently moving toward your goal, enjoying the small victories along the way, and *living the dream*, you should always have something exciting coming up: be it something to do, a location to explore, or maybe the convenience of being in a financial position to purchase an item you have had your eye on.

The point I'm making here is that living in that state of *positive expectation* isn't about obtaining one big thing: it's a series of smaller things. In fact, your life should never be void of something exciting in the near future. As you read this book, ask yourself a couple of honest questions:

1) Do my days just feel like one day leads into the next?

2) Am I so focussed on my long-term goal that I spare no regard to short-term accomplishments?

I am not trying to take away from the significance of your mental commitment to long term goals; I'm just saying that I interact with many people who are too focussed on the big picture. They end up missing out on where life really takes place: in the smaller, day-to-day activities. It is the magic of enjoying the smaller successes of every day, because *something exciting always lies ahead.*

I would recommend that, as you travel down the path toward your ultimate goal, you take the time to enjoy the small accomplishments along the way. Every day, look forward to that item that is just on the horizon. You have a life to live today, not just the one that exists in the future.

Evaluate What You Have

As a business coach, I have the opportunity to work with a lot of business people. It's very common for them to share with me their dreams and aspirations: the places they would like to go, the things that they would one day like to own, and, of course, the people they would like to help along the way.

After patiently listening to what they would describe as their perfect future, it is my job to assist them in implementing a logical plan geared toward achieving those exact results. I always start by asking, "What do we have right now?"

The response is always interesting: there is such a focus on getting somewhere else that we tend to lose sight of where we are right now. In fact, what we bring to the table is part of the fuel required to get us to that place where we want to be.

It's very common for clients to respond with, "Right now I'm nowhere. I need to get somewhere." There is no doubt I will assist them in their quest; however, I invariably must inform them that they are being unfair with themselves. They are certainly not starting from a standstill. Instead of creating something new, we are looking to enhance characteristics, attributes, and situations that they currently possess.

If this wasn't true—if all our goals, dreams, and aspirations were one hundred percent foreign to us—then that would mean that the goal we have our eye on wouldn't be an improved version of ourselves; it would be a whole new self. In other words, the ambition to become someone else.

I'm obviously a huge supporter of self-improvement, and I've invested the majority of my adult life working on myself in order to guide others down the same path. Being the best "you" isn't just a good idea: you are crazy if you don't want to spend time perfecting yourself.

That is exactly why my first question is always, "What do you have right now?" How my client answers that question tells me who they are; it tells me that they are committed to improving.

How you answer will shed some light on your own personal values, attributes, and concerns. Always living in a state of *positive expectation* makes it easier to understand where that improvement can come from; you are always *counting your blessings,* and thus know your strengths.

Sometimes, people just can't come up with anything; there is nothing about themselves or their situations that they want to hold onto. Their thought is, "Let's build something new." The problem with this thinking is it's not personal improvement—it is, in fact, building something completely different. It is turning you into someone else; to become something you're not.

The point of personal development is to discover your strengths and weaknesses: to improve on your strengths and eliminate the weak areas. You shouldn't be on a quest to become someone else: what you really need is to become the "you" 2.0.

That's why it's so important to *evaluate what you have* right now. Know who you are as a person, what skills you bring to the table, or what tools you can bring to the job site. If you *count your blessings,* you should already know what these strengths are, and can thus *evaluate what you have.*

Maybe it's true that you are in a sad state, and the improvement you have in mind is massive; however, you are still improving "you." Not trying to create a whole new person that isn't you.

Unfortunately, many people attempt to abandon who they are in search of someone who only exists in their mind. Those people can read books all day long, and attend as many seminars as they want, but they will never become someone else.

Sometimes, it may appear on the outside that they have, in fact, accomplished the task; however, it would be superficial: the inside always tells the story.

Don't try to become someone else. To be a better "you," start with *evaluating what you have*.

Dealing With the Fear of Loss

Living with a fear of loss is the opposite of living in *positive expectation*. When a person is living with the expectation that things will work out overall—the firm belief that, yes, life has an ebb and flow—they are aware that awesome things are always on the horizon. The opposite to that frame of mind is living in a constant *fear of loss*.

Most of my clients are realtors. I always find it fascinating how realtors are notorious for making this mistake. However, given the competitiveness of the industry, they are easily seduced into the *fear of loss*.

I was talking to a realtor the other day, and I enquired as to why he would have his cell number on his business card, yard signs, and his website. His response was, "If I don't call them back right away, if I'm not twenty-four-seven, then someone else will call them. I could lose the lead."

This is a classic example of operating in a *fear of loss*. Unfortunately, that mindset is not conducive to success. In fact, the fear of loss only enhances the loss element in your brain, bringing you more and more loss.

This brings us back to the concept *you become what you think about.* That the motivation is of trying *not* to lose something is inconsequential; in the brain, the main thought is loss, thus creating more loss.

If you are living in a state of *positive expectation*, then it is easier for you to avoid this cycle of fearing loss. How can you fear the negative when you see positive on the horizon?

However, like this realtor, you must be blatantly honest with yourself. If you are making decisions based on the fear of loss, you will, in fact, receive more loss.

Let's look at an example that isn't a business situation, but rather on the personal side of life. Let's say you find yourself making decisions in your relationships that, in your mind, would keep the other person interested in you. You must be honest with yourself and admit that you are operating from a *fear of loss*. I'm sure you have, at some point, observed this kind of reality, so I don't have to tell you that this will never work.

Living in *positive expectation* is the total opposite: a complete one-eighty. Living every day in the absolute expectation that awesome things are just around the next corner is dramatically different from structuring every day around the chance of losing something. Having a personal *Success Explosion* in all the aspects of your life, while still trying to hold on to the mindset of a *fear of loss,* is like someone spraying you with a hose on a hot day, and you continually try to grab the water.

Keeps Things in Perspective

Keeping things in perspective is a main ingredient in the success stew; living in a constant state of *positive expectation* will assist us in this endeavour. There is no doubt that life has a habit of sending us unwanted situations. Some of those unwelcomed guests are serious in nature, and others are nothing more than a temporary inconvenience. When a serious event presents itself, we have no option other than to deal with it in a direct fashion.

However, when a challenge comes our way that is more of a temporary nature, our constant mindset of living in that optimal state of *positive expectation* will better allow us to handle the incoming nuisance in the temporary state it was delivered.

As we travel down this amazing road called life, there is no doubt that challenges are inevitable. Some will be big, and some will be small; the trick is to manage them in the state in which they are presented.

If they are of the bigger variety, don't minimize them: use all your power to conquer them and put them in the rear-view mirror.

On the other hand, if they present themselves as smaller challenges, treat them as such: don't overreact and elevate them to a status that they don't deserve. They are on the minor list. Keep them there, and get them in the rearview mirror as quickly as possible.

We have all made the mistake of overreacting to a smaller challenge, thus increasing its profile and eventually adding it to the major list. Although we know that was a mistake, we can't do anything about it now.

However, we can be careful not to make that same mistake in the future. When we live in a constant state of *positive expectation*, we are afforded the luxury of *keeping things in perspective*.

I know this sounds like a small thing, but it's not. Save your energy for life's major challenges; don't waste it on the minor items.

Therapy for the Soul

I know this sounds a bit crazy, but it's true: living with positive expectation is therapy for the soul.

When life delivers a major blow, it takes a chip out of you; it's been said that life is a contact sport. Over time, that chip will heal. Not to say that some hurts or disappointments won't continue to exist long-term; of course they will. However, the majority of the pain will be felt when the bite is first inflicted.

During that time, it can sometimes be difficult to maintain life's daily balance. Over time, routines and your daily focus will return to normal; the point is to have as few scenarios as possible requiring this process.

When things happen that are not in the critical category, they are *therapy for the soul*. To keep them in perspective, dispense with them quickly and avoid the majority of the mental healing process.

Allows You to Laugh More

I live by many rules. One of which is when things happen, I ask myself a question: "Am I going to laugh about this later?" If the answer is "yes," then I laugh now.

Over the years, there have been many situations where this occurs. Others around me are often a little puzzled with my response to the situation. They misinterpret my laughing as me not caring about what has happened.

To them, I simply explain my reasoning: would it make sense to get all stressed out about something that I know I will laugh about later? No. So I should get over it now, and save myself that worry in the interim.

It really doesn't take long to get people on my side; everyone can think of days when implementing this practice would have come in handy.

For example, perhaps your children did something that they should not have. As a parent, you are responsible to teach them the correct path. Before you inflict whatever punishment you deem necessary, pause and ask yourself a question. "Is this something that I'm going to tell my friends and laugh about at a later date?"

If "yes," you might want to skip all the drama and laugh now. Don't get me wrong: I'm not saying skip the punishment. If they made a mistake, good parenting would say that we should take the opportunity that has been put in front of us to teach a lesson.

The punishment may be required, but the drama is not. So many people mentally buy into situations that are not really that big of a deal, and as a result make decisions that could have long-term consequences, only to then laugh about it later.

When you live every day in a state of *positive expectation,* avoiding that step is so much easier. The mindset created by always expecting awesome things coming your way makes you so much more resilient.

So when something happens that is not on the extreme list, your mind immediately spins the thought, "Compared to the life I have, this item is not really that big of a deal. In fact, I'm probably going to laugh about this later, so I might as well laugh now."

Think about how amazing that is: your mind is in the perfect state to handle a small setback. So start with laughing, then proceed to fixing: no drama, no dwelling, but lots of laughter.

In a Nutshell

Living a life of *positive expectation* allows you to take life's ups and downs in stride. We all want to be viewed as a leader, rather than be given the tag of a follower.

When we spend our days with that absolute expectancy that something awesome will happen today, we free ourselves up to afford the amazing opportunity to view each and every day as something significant. Each day is something of importance, something that should be held in high esteem.

Today is another amazing day, one that should not be taken lightly. Spend each day excited and optimistic, with the absolute expectation that it will deliver something amazing.

Helpful Exercise

Living your days in a constant state of *positive expectation* is the way to live: I don't think anyone would prefer to spend their days focussing on everything going wrong.

However, although we agree that casting our attention upon the expectation of good things is a good idea, most people take the wrong route. They fill their heads all day long with the list of what's not working. This exercise will assist you in the proper daily focus.

List three things that you would like to have happen in your life in the next twelve months.

Awesome Expectation #1: _____

Awesome Expectation #2: _____

Awesome Expectation #3: _____

It's important to understand that *we become what we think about*, not what we are *supposed* to think about or *want* to think about. Let's start giving awesome things that we want in our lives priority in our brains, and think about them all day long.

"Don't lower your expectations to meet your performance. Raise your performance to meet your expectations."

Ralph Marston

Seven

Embrace Change

There is a common saying that only three things are guaranteed: death, taxes, and change. I don't think any of them are going away any time soon, so it's best we learn how to manage them.

Death is inevitable, and as for taxes…well, that's another book altogether. For this book, let's take a look at the topic of *embracing change.*

If you take a look at the last couple hundred years, no matter what country you live in, nothing has stayed the same. Everything changes; in fact, the speed of change is rapidly increasing, and will only continue to do so. The most astute plan for us would be to stop fighting progress, and jump on that train.

Every change creates opportunity. Most people wallow in whatever change has presented itself, but visionary minds look for the opportunity that always accompanies change.

Opportunity and change travel together: you can't have one without the other. When along comes a change in your life, be it business or personal, look closely: opportunity is close by. They work as a team.

Unfortunately, most people are so overwhelmed by change that they don't see opportunity standing off in the shadows. You can't have one without the other, so let's take look at why we should *embrace change*.

It Will Change You

What I mean here is that change is inevitable. You either wilfully accept change or it changes you; either way, change is going to happen, and only one of you is going to be in control.

Either you welcome this change that has entered your life, and are purposefully looking for opportunity, or you are being traumatized by your unwelcomed visitor.

The thing with opportunity is it's only a little patient: it will hang around for a while, waiting to be discovered, but at some point it will disappear into the shadows and be gone forever.

Unfortunately, the vast majority of people spend way too much time stressing about their new, altered situation, and never notice opportunity standing off to the side. That opportunity will hang around for a bit, but at some point it moves along.

The visionary mind, the mind that *embraces change,* thinks slightly differently: it's on the look-out for opportunity. When one of life's little alterations presents itself, immediately the visionary mind is on the hunt for the opportunity that is lurking somewhere nearby.

When the visionary mind finds the opportunity, the light bulb goes on, and the opportunity can be explored. That is the dramatic difference between them and those that wallow in their life's alteration.

We know change is inevitable, so we might as well be on the right side of it. Either you are going to be in control, or change is going to control you; there is no third option.

Opportunity for Personal Growth

Personal growth is an amazing thing, one which everyone should desire. There shouldn't be an instance in anyone's life where *opportunity for personal growth* is off the table. If you have lost your pull toward personal growth, if the drive to improve yourself in all the aspects of your life is no longer important to you, get it back.

This should be your mission until the day you die: to be your best at whatever you put your hand to. It just so happens that *embracing change* is a perfect *opportunity for personal growth;* as a matter of fact, personal growth is a by-product of *embracing change.*

When the visionary mind, the mind that embraces change, encounters a life-altering moment, the immediate search for opportunity begins. This process, albeit uncommon for some people, is them stretching themselves. It is, in fact, personal growth.

It would be great if when the couple, change and opportunity, came your way, opportunity presented itself before change. Unfortunately, it doesn't work that way. Change comes first: only then can you begin a quest to find the opportunity hidden within it.

I know it would be better if it were the other way around; unfortunately, I don't make up the rules: I just explain them.

Progress

A synonymous word for progress is "change." It's going to happen, with or without you. There is no way to stop progress—not that you would if you could. Think about it: every change, every advancement, comes with a built-in opportunity. Why would you not want that?

For the rest of your life, change will continue to happen. *Progress* will, without a doubt, be evident in your life, which also means that opportunity will be present as well.

I think that you should want more opportunity. In fact, the more the better. You should be a person desiring massive change, *progress*, in your life. The saying, "Every day is full of opportunity," also means that every day is full of change; they travel together.

At some point, your life will be over. I hope you will be able to feel like you lived it as someone who embraced change: someone who was part of *progress*, and who automatically looked for opportunity, the silver lining to every cloud of change, that life brought your way.

New and Exciting Experiences

Embracing change automatically leads to new and exciting experiences. Keep in mind that every single change, in every aspect of your life, is accompanied by its closest friend: opportunity. If you consciously choose to *embrace change* and pursue the subsequent opportunity, you have chosen the path of *new and exciting experiences*.

On the other hand, if you are overwhelmed by the change or pay no attention to the following opportunity, you create a "woe is me" lifestyle, one squarely focussed on how the presented change will affect your life in a negative fashion.

The unfortunate reality is that most people fall into this category; they live their lives as if they are always the victim. Sometimes in life, horrible things do happen, and referring to yourself as the victim is merely a statement of fact.

However, what we're talking about here is life's everyday, run-of-the-mill change: the change we are supposed to embrace in order to immediately hunt down the opportunity that's hiding in plain sight. When we do that, when we capture that opportunity, it's a guarantee that a *new and exciting experience* is about to occur.

Of course, that also means that if we perceive the change as a negative impact on our lives, it will rob us of the new and exciting experience that is right there for the taking.

Makes us Strong

It's been said that, "What doesn't kill you makes you stronger." There is some truth to that. It's true that advancing makes you stronger, and retreating makes you weaker. Although occasionally retreating, whether physically or mentally, makes sense for many reasons, we become both physically and mentally stronger when we are advancing.

As an example, if you damage a muscle while exercising, it makes sense to stop working the affected area and let it heal. Even though that is the correct course of action, during that time you are not getting stronger; at least, not physically. That only happens when you are working the muscle.

When change happens and you automatically begin the search for opportunity, you are instinctively advancing. That pursuing nature is what makes you strong; when you are strong, you are more durable than the average person.

The opposite would be to continually fold up like a cheap tent every time the slightest thing happens. This, in turn, makes you vulnerable.

I think we should all aspire to being strong, both physically and mentally. Fortunately, because change is constant and opportunity is its travel partner, life gives us plenty of chances to exercise both mental and physical toughness.

Every time we encounter a change, we have another chance to stretch ourselves. It is another opportunity to push ourselves to another level: the process that builds strength and character. It's like working out for your brain.

Be More Flexible

Embracing change is an excellent way to become more flexible. In nature, a tree that is rigid will eventually break in the wind, while a flexible one will bend and survive. I'm not talking about being physically flexible. I'm talking about mental flexibility: the ability to roll with the punches and easily handle life's daily ups and downs.

If you do not possess a flexible nature, having a *Success Explosion* would be virtually impossible. You would spend most of your days dealing with life's little obstacles, stuck in an inflexible frame of mind. I know that I don't have to convince you that this simply will not work.

Fortunately, when you *embrace change* you automatically become a more flexible person. *Being flexible* is a natural by-product of *embracing change,* and both are a necessary piece in the success puzzle.

These are all great reasons why it's important to *embrace change.* Now let's take a look at how you can master it.

Be Patient

Things often take longer than we sometimes have patience for; in fact, the process is almost always beyond the time commitment that most people are willing to invest. Since change is one of life's unavoidable absolutes, it makes sense to be the one in control of it.

My concern is that the natural impatience of most people prevents them from accomplishing this. They feel the need to *go from zero to hero.* I must caution you that mastering the ability to embrace change is like everything: it takes time to get good at it.

Patience is the key: it is unrealistic to hold yourself to such a high standard that you expect yourself to be able to perfectly embrace change as soon as you agree that it's a good idea. Like all things, we will not be good at it until we have done it for a while.

Riding a bike is pretty basic: I'm sure you can do it. However, in the beginning you probably had training wheels. Then, once they were removed, a few scraped knees.

Looking for the opportunity in change is just like that: you are probably not going to be very good at it in the beginning. However, you must continue to hone the skill and master it, even when you stumble and, occasionally, fail.

The first time you fell off a bike, you didn't pack it in; you didn't say that it's too difficult. Almost everyone can ride a bike, and all of them completed that task despite the bruises and skinned knees.

Over time, you will become much better at finding opportunity. It's not a game of hide-and-seek; or if it is, opportunity isn't a very good player, because it never hides. So be patient, because you will eventually develop the skill. The good news is there are plenty of opportunities to practice, since change is so very common.

Doubt is Natural

Don't allow yourself to believe that *embracing change* is for others and not for you. Doubt is natural: everyone experiences it.

When I work with business people, it's amazing how often they fully agree with principles like accepting change and then tell me a story about how they are somehow exempt from it. That, in some way, their situation is different.

Principles like how change and opportunity are constant companions are universal; no situation or scenario is exempt in any way.

It would be very unfortunate if you somehow, someway, doubted your way into never achieving the art of *embracing change*; if your lifetime was fulfilled and all you ever knew was how change had affected you, without experiencing the opportunity that travels with it. Sadly, many people do.

Doubt is natural; just don't let it be in control, or worse, be permanent.

Wallowing is Counterproductive

Wallowing is a sad state, yet most of the residents of planet Earth live in it. Why would they choose to live a depressed life? In reality, it's a natural progression that occurs if we don't *embrace change* and its partner, opportunity.

I think we can agree that, on a regular basis, change is in the cards for us. The non-visionary mind will react in a negative way, and then continues to live on in that state of mind.

Along comes another change; now, we have a new perceived problem with the previous perceived problem still percolating in our brain.

Not too far down the road, a third change reveals itself; now we are processing three perceived problems, and before you know it, we say to someone, "Oh my gosh; when it rains, it pours!"

If you think it through, this process could, and should, have gone quite differently:

That first change comes your way. Perhaps they cut your hours at work. So you begin to seek out change's travel partner, and realize that this would be an excellent opportunity to improve your education. Recognizing the opportunity to improve yourself in the grand scheme of things, you do exactly that.

Next you get a call from your child's school. Your 10-year-old son got in a fight, and is suspended for three days. Once again, you look for opportunity, and realize this would be a perfect chance for a child-parent learning experience.

A couple days later, your partner decides that this relationship isn't working for them, and you are on your own. After you digest the situation, you realize that some time to yourself—getting back to who you really are—wouldn't be such a bad idea. The situation is still a bad one, but you've taken the opportunity that has presented itself and not added it on to the previous negative situations.

I've just explained three common changes that were acted upon positively, using the opportunity presented along with the change. But each opportunity could only be acted upon because it was sought out. As a result, we have more time thanks to the decreased work hours to pursue advancing our education, the heart-to-heart we had with our 10-year-old was long overdue, and the additional time to ourselves is refreshing thanks to the breakup.

On the other hand, if we don't look for the opportunity in each of these common scenarios, we could find ourselves stressing about the reduced work hours, doubting ourselves as a parent because of our child's scrap at school, and then on top of it all the breakup: "When it rains, it pours."

I don't intend to make light of life's challenges; I'm just pointing out that opportunity and change travel together. *Wallowing is counterproductive.* It's no way to live your life.

Go Easy on Yourself

People have a habit of being too hard on themselves. I commonly say to an audience, "You know you are not perfect," to which they whole-heartedly agree. Then why do we pretend that we are?

Everyone would agree that they are not perfect; and yet people seem to hold themselves to that scale of perfection. We need to cut ourselves some slack, and allow ourselves the time required to perfect the skill of looking for opportunity in life's constant challenges.

If we don't accept that some trial and error is necessary, we could deprive ourselves of the desired result. Being impatient with yourself is a common habit that you need to kick; it's just a hindrance to the process.

Commit, Don't Just "Try"

I teach hundreds of seminars annually, and although it's rare for me to encounter someone who disagrees with the principle of *embracing change*, what I find interesting is how many people whole-heartedly agree, and then respond with, "I'll give it a try."

As Yoda once told Luke, "Try not! Do ... or do not. There is no try."

Getting to where you want to go will require a lot more than the "I'll give it a try" mindset. To have a *Success Explosion* in your life will require an "I *will* do it" mindset.

We must commit and create determination in our spirit. Failure cannot be an option. We must embrace change, and subsequently hunt down the opportunity that is also present. Which means more than casually looking around to see if opportunity will jump out in front of you and scream, "Here I am—over here!" It doesn't work that way.

Opportunity is definitely present, but you must seek it out. This will ensure that you will experience personal growth in the process.

Personal growth is an amazing thing; I am so glad that opportunity requires it. If it were to present itself too easily, it would rob me of the growth I experience while searching.

So be persistent. If change has come into your life, opportunity is also present. Be thankful that opportunity will require effort on your behalf, because without it, you would not grow.

In a Nutshell

Embracing constant change is one of the most liberating attributes a person can possess. Acknowledge that change and opportunity are an inseparable pair. Then the trick is to manage your mindset when change comes your way.

Instead of viewing the presented change as a negative, train your brain to search for the opportunity that is surely hanging around close by. You will have to search for it, to allow for the growth process, but it is also not so hidden that discovery is impossible.

Because change is so common, we have many occasions to practise this principle. Life is amazing; I hope you have the patience to learn how to make the jump from being affected by change to embracing it, and taking advantage of the opportunities it presents.

Helpful Exercise

Change is inevitable; the real question isn't whether or not it will happen, it's how we will deal with our new situation.

When a change presents itself, we have a choice to view it as a glass half-full or a glass half-empty. We can look at the benefits of our new environment, or focus on our perceived losses; it's our choice.

Purposefully seeking out the benefits of our new situation is the mentally healthier way to go.

To help you practice doing just that, list three changes you are currently experiencing and two positive benefits connected to your new scenario.

Recent Change #1:

Benefit #1:

Benefit #2:

Recent Change #2:

Benefit #1:

Benefit #2:

Recent Change #3:

Benefit #1:

Benefit #2:

It's all about perspective!

"*Your life does not get better by chance, it gets better by change.*"

Jim Rohn

Eight
A Determined Spirit

In our quest for a bona fide *Success Explosion*, determination is essential. Implementing any of this book's chapters would be quite difficult without the required level of determination.

Being a determined person will allow you to achieve everything discussed in this book; actually, being a determined person is what will allow you to achieve anything you have read in *any* book.

Determination is the attribute that makes all good ideas become reality. Determination is that voice within you that screams, "That's it—that's what I have been looking for. That's the direction I should be heading."

Determination doesn't give you the destination; it gives you the means of getting there. For example, let's say you decide to drive somewhere. You own a car, so that's good; however, you don't have any gas. You know where you want to go, and you have the means of transportation, but unfortunately, you still can't get there. All you need is the gas, and although that doesn't sound like much, without it, you are undeniably stuck.

I meet people all the time that tell me where in life they would love to go; in many cases, the destination has been charted for years. They know the where, they possess the means, but what they don't have is *a determined spirit* to get going.

If you want to travel to Montréal, plan your route, gas up, and go. If your destination is in one of the worthwhile goals in your life, chart your course, gas up with determination, and let's get going.

Just like the literal gas that will take you to Montréal, the metaphorical gas of *determination* will power you toward whatever goal you set.

Physically driving to Montréal will probably be event-free, without any mishaps along the way. However, the path to achieving a goal isn't quite like that. If it were, determination wouldn't be so high on the success priority list.

It's a pretty good bet that, along the road to achieving a life goal, there will be some bumps—maybe some big ones. I'm willing to take that bet and say that the road to achieving a worthwhile goal will rarely be smooth.

So when these expected obstacles occur, our *determined spirit* is what kicks in to propel us toward our desired destination. The more frequent the bumps, the more we have to dig down to access our reservoir of determination to push ourselves faster and faster toward the finish line.

You might be thinking, "That doesn't sound like how it goes for me when I hit obstacles along the way." The ability to dig down and access enormous reservoirs of determination isn't easy for many people, which would explain why so few actually experience a *Success Explosion* in all areas of their lives.

Don't fool yourself: there are many people that the word "determined" describes to a "T." And for them, what I described is exactly what they do: dig down to the depths of their inner spirit and draw on that abundance of determination that continually resides there.

This book is about being aware of the required attributes to experience a *Success Explosion* and having the determination to collect all of them. Let's take a look at some of the common traits people with massive amounts of determination have in common.

They Learn From the Past

If you would like to be on the "short list" of people possessing the required amount of determination, it's important that we learn from the past and then leave it be. Not everything in our past is positive; I hope I'm not the only person who has said and done things that, in hindsight, wasn't the smartest play.

However, what's done is done; I can't change those events, so it's best to learn from them and then leave them there. Like you, I also have some accomplishments that I am very proud of; things that I look back on fondly as a positive action.

When we reflect on positive activities from our past, it's like adding gas to your engine; on the other hand, when we reflect on negative activities, it's like having a hole in your gas tank, allowing all your determination to leak out.

If something from your past is on the wrong side of the ledger, you would be wise to make peace with yourself and let it go; it is never a good idea to allow that item to become a stumbling block to all your future endeavours. Determined people don't make that mistake.

They Are Not Complainers

With over twenty years of coaching and training, it's been my observation that those who possess the necessary determination have a tendency to complain less—a lot less. When obstacles fall into their path, they skip the whining and instead latch onto the opportunity that is presented. They are of the mindset that there is no point complaining: no one cares.

The truth of this statement is a difficult one to determine. Maybe if it were, and everyone knew it, maybe we would all wallow less. I know we can always find a friend who will wallow with us; however, that's probably more an example of "misery loves company" than someone who really cares.

Those that are driven by a determined spirit are not the complainers of the planet; quite frankly, they don't have the time for it. They are so focussed on where they are going that the challenges along the way are expected and quickly dispensed with.

I find myself reminding people that they are not Velcro: everything shouldn't stick to them. The vast majority of items should fall right off. Honestly, buying into the drama of every life challenge is more a habit than anything else.

Usually I hear, "But Rob, you don't understand!" However, the truth is I do understand: I understand that there is not enough determination to take the edge off of that particular scenario.

When coaching people, I check their last week of work activity prior to the scheduled coaching call. It's common for me to observe several items that did not go their way in that week.

When I enquire after a determined person's last week, their reply is usually, "Things are going great!" I'll ask, "What about these two situations?" "Oh yes; they didn't work out. But it's all part of the process." That's how they equate setbacks.

Most of our new clients, who simply have not yet matured to that stage, want to spend the entire coaching session breaking down every aspect of that week's setbacks; it pretty much turns into a counselling session.

Determined people don't complain; their focussed nature quickly disposes of the items that did not go their way. They are not Velcro; only the good stuff sticks.

They are Forward Thinkers

No one would ever drive their car while continually looking at the rear-view mirror. That would be a very dangerous way to get around.

Life is like that as well: we shouldn't drive through life squarely focussed on the past. Like your car, your gaze should remain primarily through the windshield, and only occasionally should you glance in your rear-view mirror.

If you drove your car the other way around, spending most of your time looking in the rear-view and only occasionally glancing through the windshield, it wouldn't be long before you ran directly into an obstacle that you wouldn't have otherwise hit.

Life is the same: too much backward thinking leads to you creating your own obstacles not too far down the road. On the other hand, if you do it correctly, you would be in a position to navigate successfully to your desired destination.

Determined people are forward thinkers; they don't care about past life experiences. They have already made the realization that the balance of their lives takes place in front of their vehicle, not behind.

Constantly looking at the rear-view mirror is a dangerous way to drive: don't drive your life that way. Determined people realize that all their aspirations reside in their future, not their past.

Encouraging, Not Envious

Determined people are ecstatic when others achieve greatness; those that operate with an inadequate level of determination tend to be envious of others' accomplishments.

Those that lack determination and find themselves experiencing feelings of envy are, in most cases, envious of others because they are disappointed in themselves. They are acutely aware that envy is a poor characteristic for a person to possess, and they often work quite diligently to remove the feeling, without success.

If this is you, don't be disappointed with yourself; that's not who you are. I know you don't actually want to feel envious: it's just difficult to find a long-term solution.

The good news is it's easy to fix: just increase your levels of determination. Then you will find yourself genuinely happy when others do well, and the envious tendencies will be replaced with feelings of encouragement. But with low levels of determination, there will be no fighting those feelings of envy.

You can't fake this; either you are authentically happy and encourage others in their successes, or you are envious. There really isn't any neutral ground. Determined people have eliminated envy from their lives; you should as well.

They Are in Control

Sometimes, between business and personal situations, life can get a little hectic. Therefore, it's not uncommon to feel overwhelmed, as if you have lost control.

Although this does sometimes happen to a determined person, to them it occurs a lot less. This particular trait, of being in control, is a by-product of increasing determination.

It's always a good thing when you automatically pick up positive attributes simply by mastering others: increase your determination, and a sense of control comes as an added benefit.

If you are operating with minimal determination, the odds of you being in control are quite low; the situations that you lack the determination to overcome will undoubtedly control your day-to-day activities.

On the other hand, if you travel down the path of increased determination, you will remove your Velcro-like shell and problems simply can no longer stick to you.

Sometimes, it can appear like determined people don't care; that's not true, they just don't get attached to their problems. Their *determined spirit* is just too strong.

It's interesting, this lack of understanding between the two groups. Those that lack determination can't figure out how people with determined spirits move past things so easily. They stop and wonder, "Don't they care?"

Meanwhile, those possessing determination can't fathom why others still wallow: "That happened two weeks ago, why not move along?"

You have a choice of which group you will occupy; all that is required is to build up your determination.

Every Day is Exciting

This point, like the previous one, is simply a by-product of living with high levels of determination. It would be difficult to live your life in a state of *positive expectancy*, determined to achieve a *Success Explosion*, and not be excited all day every day.

It's so fantastic to hang around with people like this; unless, of course, you are on the other side of the fence. A person who is without determination is constantly looking in the rear-view mirror and spending most of their time being envious of other's accomplishments.

If this is you, then spending time with excited people can be quite nauseating. You would have to be brave enough to admit to yourself that you are the problem in this situation; you are the one out of sync.

A great idea would be to grab hold of massive amounts of determination and never let go; soon, you will find yourself totally excited about life. When you encounter another excited person, you will be inspired by them instead of the embarrassing envious quality you might currently possess.

Determined people are excited every day, and feed off of others of a like mind; be one of them.

Burning Desire

A burning desire is a difficult attribute to possess; some naturally do, which is quite fortunate for them. Most, like me, are required to cultivate this quality, to work to develop it.

Obtaining a burning desire, like most things in life, is a process: it takes time, and patience will be required. The burning desire you will need to possess isn't an attribute you can start with: it's one that is developed along the way.

Chapter One in this book acknowledges the need to *get over things quickly*. This trait can be made all the more difficult if we can't free ourselves from the unnecessary hurt and guilt from the past.

Although I say "unnecessary," it is not to mean that past emotions like hurt and guilt weren't valid: just that they are in the past and we should leave them there. A determined person finds it easier to look ahead, rather than behind at the things they have done that they are not proud of. They are better able to *get over it quickly.*

The ability to *get over things quickly,* combined with a *determined spirit,* will go a long way in developing a burning desire for your goal. Each of the principles of this book, and the principles contained in other great books, will assist you in obtaining that powerful, burning desire.

Once obtained, you will become that person you have been looking for: the person who creates a clear picture of their destination, and under no circumstances will ever let it go. Failure is no longer an option for you, because you will have a determined, *burning desire* driving the train.

Inner Belief

To have a true *Success Explosion* and to live in a genuine, determined state of mind, we have to possess two levels of *inner belief.* On one level, we must believe that we are deserving of the destination that we have charted. On the second level, we must believe that the destination is a worthwhile one.

Let's first consider the *inner belief* that we deserve the success. There is no doubt that I have a different take on what we deserve compared to what you will read in most other books. The modern, common theme is that you deserve it: that there is nothing, in fact, that you don't deserve.

That thinking, in my opinion, is partly what created a generation commonly known as the "generation of entitlement." It is one that claims that "you deserve it," even though you haven't necessarily done anything to get it.

I certainly know where people get this thinking from: nearly every motivational book and inspirational seminar propagates that exact message: you deserve it.

However, how we view things is vitally important. If anything, this attitude leads primarily to sitting around and doing nothing, wondering why all those things that you deserve are not coming your way.

When you think about it, it is probably a good thing that the universe doesn't work in this way. You need to possess a strong *inner belief* that you deserve your goals in order to have the determination to reach them, after all. However, I think if you are honest with yourself and your past, you would probably agree that you don't really want what you deserve.

I know that as I look at my life, I regret many things that I have said and done, and although these items are in the past—and that's where they'll stay—if life were to give me what I honestly deserve, I might not be happy with the result.

I did start this section by saying you should have an *inner belief* that you deserve the destination you have charted. But then I've gone on to say you actually don't. To be clear, I am saying that it is my firm opinion that none of us *automatically* deserve anything. Deserving quality things in your life is not a right: things don't come to you because you are entitled to them.

I do personally have a strong *inner belief* that I am deserving of my worthwhile goals, but not just because I'm born on planet Earth. It's not a birthright. However, I do acknowledge that everyone is in the same boat. Since none of us inherently deserve anything, we all "deserve" at the same level.

Therefore, you must be the one deserving of your worthwhile goal, because you are the person most determined to see it through. Because we are all in the same boat, no one is more deserving of that goal than you.

Courageous

Being courageous is such an excellent attribute for a person to possess: it is courage that drives determination.

When our minds drift to the topic of courage, we can't help but think about the courage required in battle or from a warrior in our favourite show. It's true that this is an example of courage at its peak, and I am extremely grateful to those who willingly put themselves in harm's way so that I can live in a safe society where I can actively pursue my dreams.

However, most people, myself included, will never be in that kind of life-and-death situation. Instead, in this section I'm talking about the day-to-day courage that you will need to muster in order to manage life's obstacles.

If a difficult conversation must be had, you need to exercise courage and go through with it. If you feel in your heart that you are being treated unfairly, you must generate the necessary courage and speak up.

The opposite of being a courageous person is being a cowardly person. It's important that you stand up for yourself and what you believe: become a person who speaks their mind.

I don't, in any way, mean to encourage you to be that person who is too opinionated and constantly outspoken; however, others should know where you stand.

When you lack courage, you will automatically become a person who continually procrastinates. It's a natural progression, and one that makes it difficult to be a person determinedly pursuing your bona fide *Success Explosion*.

If you worry too much about how others will perceive you, you will continue to keep your thoughts to yourself just so that you to avoid those awkward conversations.

When you have the courage to speak up, you let the world know where you stand. Although it's true that extreme courage is asked of some people, the majority will only be required to have the courage to stand up and be counted.

I know this sounds basic, but the truth is, many people lack this kind of courage and spend their lives living in the shadows. Courage drives determination!

In a Nutshell

Determination is a required element to achieve a *Success Explosion*. Be courageous on a day-to-day basis. Realize that the past is exactly that: the past. Sometimes, things don't go your way, but whether it was your fault or not at this point it is immaterial. The future is waiting for you, and you can't reach it if you're carrying around all the junk from your past.

Attack your amazing future with vigour. Mentally grab hold of it, and under no circumstances let it go.

"I am a determined person; I never give up."

Helpful Exercise

Determination is such a vital attribute for a person to possess. For some, it comes naturally. However, for most, myself included, it's a learned process.

For this exercise, let's keep it simple. Focus on just one item that you know you need to be a lot more determined about. This could be a business goal, something relationship-driven, or a health situation; either way, it should be easy for you to itemize something in your life that requires an injection of determination.

Once we itemize it, it would be wise to add a few simple action steps to get you started and then keep you on track.

Finish the following sentence:
In my life right now, I need to have a lot more determination in the following area:

To help me with this venture, I will take the following steps on a daily basis:

Action Step #1:

Action Step #2:

Action Step #3:

Think about how much better your life would be if you could complete the daily action steps. You would make the item you desire a reality!

"You can receive motivation from others, but determination is solely your responsibility."

Anonymous

Nine

The Power of Enthusiasm

Being an enthusiastic person has many benefits, and of course it's a necessary component in a *Success Explosion*.

A lot of people choose to live their lives focussed on all these situations that occupy the negative side of life's ledger. Be clear when I say, "they choose," because I mean exactly that: they have chosen to live in that state of mind.

However, when a person chooses to be enthusiastic about life, it's actually difficult to live in the same defeatist mindset that the majority of people settle for.

When we purposefully live an enthusiastic existence, we are actually living the life that we visualize as our perfect future.

Think about it: we periodically find ourselves dreaming about what life could be, at some point in the future. Considering that it is our daydream, we might as well make it perfect: so in the motion picture of our mind, we observe ourselves as perfect in every way.

In this daydream, we don't see ourselves depressed, low on energy, or moving around with a lack of confidence. We see our perfect self as, among other attributes, an energetic and enthusiastic person.

We all have an inner desire to leave the planet a better place than how we found it, and that is accomplished by being a person who understands *the power of enthusiasm.*

Enthusiasm will take you a long way down the road that you intend to travel: a long way to fulfilling that perfect motion picture running constantly in your head.

Some people feel that others can be enthusiastic because of everything that they have, and because things are always "going their way." In fact, quite the opposite is true: the enthusiasm came first. It was their enthusiasm that assisted in the appearance of having everything.

If your true desire is to live the life of the motion picture that your brain keeps playing, an enthusiastic nature is required now. Not at some point in the future: now. If you cannot find a way to be an energetic and enthusiastic person today, I'm sorry to say that the motion picture playing in your mind will never be released to theaters.

It's a Daily Choice

Some of the people that I have spoken to have convinced themselves that their circumstances have, in some way, made living in a state of enthusiasm unattainable.

I would say that, given their situation, yes, enthusiasm does not greet them automatically every morning. Instead, generating some enthusiasm will require some conscious effort. Down the road, maybe daily enthusiasm will come more easily. Like anything, it takes *patience* and a *daily choice* to learn.

I must assume that many reading this book have real issues: issues that greet you every morning, and can hinder the process of creating some bona fide enthusiasm. I have certainly had some dark days, ones where being an enthusiastic person seemed unrealistic.

If this sounds like you, I would recommend that you take some time to reflect on the things in your life that *are* currently going your way. Perhaps friends, family, or maybe your career. Once you get that mental boost, visit the movie in your head and take a mental trip into your perfect future.

As you read this book, maybe life is good for you right now, and generating enthusiasm comes naturally. That's amazing; however, in the future there will be days that you are on the other side of that coin, and taking stock of the good things in your life will be helpful.

Although being an enthusiastic person is *a daily choice*, some days will be more challenging than others. However, that does not change the fact that, if you want to actually star in the perfect movie of your life, being an enthusiastic person is mandatory.

Some days enthusiasm comes easier than others, but to happen it is still *your choice*. Likewise, if you spend your days moping around, that too is your choice, not something your situation has created for you.

It's Infectious

There is no doubt that, as we travel through our days, we affect our surroundings, either in a positive or a negative fashion. It would be unrealistic to think that our attitude could have no effect on our environment; in fact, we have much more influence than we give ourselves credit for.

Any day completed in an enthusiastic manner has a positive impact on those around you; the greater the enthusiasm, the greater the impact.

It can be difficult to gauge your impact; perhaps someone you interact with picks up on your enthusiasm, and realizes that something affecting them isn't as devastating as they first thought. Because of your *daily choice* to exercise *the power of enthusiasm*, you inadvertently alter their day in a positive manner.

Unfortunately, every coin has two sides, which also means the opposite is true: if you purposefully choose not to exercise enthusiasm, that same interaction could inadvertently push that person deeper in the wrong direction.

I'm not saying that you are responsible for others' mindsets; I'm just pointing out that you are responsible for your own, and the choice you make will influence not only your own situation, but also those of others surrounding you.

Over time, being an enthusiastic person will become a habit, and you will notice that others will be drawn to you. This is because by being enthusiastic, you are purposefully being the opposite of everyone else: you stand out as the different one. There is so much negative in the world: too many people have made a conscious choice not to operate their daily life using *the power of enthusiasm*.

It's true that, at first, some people may find you annoying for your enthusiasm. I have experienced this myself. To understand this annoyance, you must first understand the process people go through when change is necessary.

The first, most common emotion is denial. Eventually, they may move on to acceptance. But when another person finds your enthusiasm a little irritating, they are really experiencing the emotion of denial. With your influence, it won't be too far down the line that they will arrive at the acceptance stage.

You have a choice each and every day to affect your surroundings in either a positive or negative fashion. It's important that you don't let a few things that are not quite going your way affect that process.

If having a *Success Explosion* is your desire, then enthusiasm is required of you every day.

Makes You a Leader

There are really only two categories here: a leader or a follower. If you ask one hundred people, "Are you a leader, or a follower?" the vast majority would quickly respond, "Leader, for sure."

Deep down, we all want to be a leader. Now, I'm not necessarily talking about the level of leader who is running an organization or company—although that, of course, would be fine if that's the position you find yourself in. If this is you, you have drawn many people to you with your *infectious enthusiasm* in days past.

What I'm really talking about is being a leader at your sphere of influence. This is the level where most people exercise their leadership skills.

If you wonder whether you are, in fact, viewed as a leader among your peer group, ask yourself a couple of questions:

1) Am I the person people go to when they need advice or input, particularly when it has the potential to significantly alter their future?

2) When the chips are down in a stressful situation, do others turn to me for direction? In other words, do they view me as the logical person to take control? Am I viewed as the conduit for a solution?

Enthusiasm is characteristic of a leader. It causes you to emanate a subconscious message: "You can follow me—I know the way. And if I don't know already, I will find it; you are safe with me."

What I'm explaining here is not an ego thing: it's not an "I must be in control" issue. It's more of a quiet confidence created by, among other attributes, the ability to create enthusiasm on a daily basis.

Grants the Courage to Be Bold

Operating all your days with a proper dose of enthusiasm creates a healthy form of boldness.

"Boldness" is an interesting word: it can be used to somehow mean that you are impudent or out of line, but I don't mean it that way. I'm talking about the form of boldness that is connected to courage.

When you navigate each day with enthusiasm, you will automatically force yourself outside of your personal comfort zone. I know that the comfort zone is a comfortable place—that's why they call it that—but unfortunately, you can't grow from there. Everything you want is outside of your comfort zone, and it's with the getting out and exploring of life's opportunities that your boldness will be called upon.

Given that most people have trouble getting out of that so-comfortable comfort zone, where everything appears safe, finding the courage to exercise enthusiasm to experience exactly the opposite on a daily basis can be quite difficult.

However, day after day of constant enthusiasm will make it virtually impossible to confine yourself to that perceived safe zone. It would be like trying to fit back into the clothes you wore as a youth—you have simply outgrown them. Going back is now impossible.

If you try to push together two magnets with matching poles, it won't matter how hard you try; they won't stay together. Likewise, when you demonstrate enthusiasm on a daily basis, you won't be able to retreat back into your comfort zone. Even if you tried, it would simply push you out.

The enthusiastic nature you have cultivated over time will have created so much positive boldness that the comfort zone will somehow feel like the uncomfortable place. There is a saying: "Ships are safe in harbours, but they are not made for there."

We are the same way: we are safe in our comfort zone, but we are not made to be there all the time. We are designed to be out where the waves can be rough, where the weather has the potential to be turbulent, and where we can take advantage of our carefully-built fortifications, like a strong ship on the ocean.

If ships could talk, oh the stories they would tell: all the places they have been, the exotic locales, the conquered storms, maybe even the attacks by pirates. We should get out of the harbour and create our own amazing stories—maybe minus the pirates!

On the other hand, if you push two magnets together with opposite poles, they rush to each other. From there, the strength of the magnets dictates how challenging it is to separate them.

That's exactly how it is with a person who purposefully avoids living in a state of enthusiasm. A sense of boldness is not created, and the comfort zone is like a magnet that continually draws them back in to perceived safety.

Due to the lack of generated boldness that person will, in all likelihood, settle in to the perceived safety of the comfort zone, and the magnet's hold increases.

As you read this, you are probably thinking, "It would be a shame to choose to live in the harbour instead of the high seas, where all the adventure is." You would be correct: that is a shame. However, this is exactly where most people live, in the crowded harbour.

The high seas are wide open, and that is where leaders choose to patrol: outside the perceived comfort zone. Meanwhile, followers live in the harbour and admire the leaders from afar.

It makes no sense to fortify a ship and then simply park it in a harbour for its life; it equally makes no sense for a person, who is even more prepared for adventure, to choose to complete their existence in the perceived safety of the comfort zone.

You were created to be a leader, just like a ship was created to seek adventure. It would be a shame to choose the role of follower when the adventure of life is calling for a leader.

You might notice that I have used the phrase "perceived safety" in reference to the comfort zone. This is because hurricanes destroy ships in harbours all the time. They are safer there, for sure, but not invulnerable.

Live in a state of healthy boldness: get out of the harbour and be the leader that you were intended to be.

Become a Success Magnet

Becoming a *success magnet* certainly does sound like an interesting proposition: to actually be magnetic to success. I'm pleased to inform you that this is exactly what millions of people experience on a daily basis. And enthusiasm, although not the sole reason, is definitely the primary one.

When we purposefully choose to live our lives in a state of enthusiasm, we automatically improve our position to that of a glass-half-full kind of person. Because *we become what we think about*, when we lean toward the positive, we attract more of the same. We attract positive situations, scenarios, and people.

We begin to architect our own perfect circumstances; we are magnetic to everything that we want, and repel those negative items that are attracted to those who are glass-half-empty people.

This is an automatic process; if enthusiasm is among your natural qualities, then you would naturally attract what you are truly after. On the other hand, the opposite is equally as powerful: if your personal characteristics are negative, then you will automatically be attracted to those same items that you are trying to avoid.

The subconscious mind does not really have a preference; if you choose to be negative, it doesn't think, "Oh that's too bad; the positive would have been a better choice." It just completes its job with absolute perfection, making you magnetic toward whatever you are thinking.

You will notice as you read this book that I constantly say that you have a choice. You consciously choose which direction your life is heading. *Adversity will happen*; I'm not saying that you have control over every aspect of life. I'm just pointing out that you have the control to choose the direction.

This means that when you choose to travel down the positive path, negative things will still happen. However, your life will be mostly positive. Conversely, if you choose the negative route, positive things will still happen, but negativity will be the dominant player.

You have a choice, so I would highly recommend that you choose to make enthusiasm a defining characteristic. In turn, you will be making yourself a *success magnet*.

Improves Health

When we think about overall health, our mind tends to think about exercise and what we put into our bodies—for good reason. In our ever-expanding world of marketing, we are inundated with exercise equipment and new fad diets. Don't get me wrong: I'm all for continual exercise and proper eating habits.

However, we tend to forget the third piece of the puzzle: the way we think. The number of commercials we see on television, hear on the radio, or view on the internet about this topic lean overwhelmingly toward physical exertion and proper eating habits. We see perfectly-shaped people in peak condition working out on newly-invented body sculpting apparatuses, drinking shakes made from the latest super foods.

As I was writing this chapter, I paused to think about the last time I had seen or heard an advertisement promoting a healthy brain. I actually spent quite a bit of time pondering this question, and could not come up with any examples. I'm not saying that they are not out there; I just couldn't come up with one.

Take a minute and think about the marketing that has reached you in regard to your physical body. Then think about something that has reached you in regard to your food intake or control.

Now try to think about a marketing campaign that focussed on the health benefits of thinking correctly, or those connected to living with *the power of enthusiasm.* You might find yourself just like me: staring into space and racking your brain, but still coming up blank.

Again, I'm not saying information and programs on the health benefits of living enthusiastically don't exist; I'm just saying that compared to the other two, your physical body and what you eat seem to have a greater priority in the media.

Interesting that, of the three, a person's ability to think is the most important by a long shot. Which begs the question: why is it the least addressed? Well, I guess marketers can sell you a piece of equipment to obtain a chiselled body—guaranteed—or have you become a life-time subscriber to a nutrition program, but not a product to increase enthusiasm.

If you're like me and you want to be healthy, you may own a universal gym which you are committed to using regularly, or adhere to nutritional guidelines that found their way to you via the previously-mentioned marketing campaigns.

The point I'm making is that the most important of these three is the positive way you think, and the health benefits connected to being an enthusiastic person.

When it comes to living as a healthy person, it would be unwise to focus on your muscles and nutrition and neglect the most powerful part of your body: the brain. When your brain is thinking correctly, when you are living under *the power of enthusiasm*, the other two will be a lot easier to stick with. In an enthusiastic state, you will be much more likely to complete your required workouts and adhere to your personal eating guidelines.

It would be a shame if someone were to only focus on their outward person, the body, while at the same time bringing all sorts of stress, doubts, and fears into their daily life. They may possess the perfect body on the outside, but they could still suffer from multiple internal challenges.

In a perfect world, we would instead adhere to physical health and nutritional guidelines, all the while allowing our brain to be a part of the healthy process.

A Life Well-Lived

At the end of the day, I think we are all looking for *a life well lived.* At some point, we will all breathe our last. People will gather for a celebration and reflect on our lives.

I would hope that, when it is my turn, the theme will be *a life well lived.* I would like people to reflect on my positive attitude, the contributions I made to my fellow man, and the things I accomplished, both business-wise and personal. I would like my commitment to my faith to be mentioned, along with all the cool stuff that I did.

It's important to me that it's not a sad occasion; I truly want everyone to come to the realization that "Wow, this was *a life well lived.*"

I believe most people, at their core, are the same. When it is their time to go, they would want everyone to come to the realization that theirs was *a life well lived.*

What do we have to do for others to consider ours *a life well lived?* It's a progression: day after day of displaying your positive characteristics for all to see. Carry that enthusiastic nature to everyone you encounter on a daily basis.

Think about what your life will look like if you project your positive outlook year after year. Think about the places you'll go, the things you'll do, and the goals you will accomplish.

The more you apply the concepts of this book, the more you will expand your personal horizons, and the further you will distance yourself from that pesky comfort zone.

It would be difficult to accomplish the goal of *a life well lived* if you spent your time residing inside your comfort zone. By implementing *the power of enthusiasm,* you make it virtually impossible for the comfort zone to keep a hold of you.

When your time does come, and others gather to pay

their respects, if you lived your life outside the comfort zone, there are those that will say, "Yes: theirs was a life well lived."

I think you should give some serious consideration to this topic. I think that if you were to consider your life in all honesty, you may have to admit that if your time was up today, others might not be able to say that yours was *a life well lived.*

If this is you, I implore you not to waste another day: get some positive enthusiasm and quickly run out of your comfort zone. Life is amazing: get out there and experience it. Participate in *a life well lived.*

In a Nutshell

Living with enthusiasm is a conscious decision; the benefits are numerous. In this chapter, we explored several; however, there are many more. I may have made enthusiasm one chapter, but others have written entire books on why living with enthusiasm is so important. Even still, we could not cover all the benefits.

So in this book, I endeavour to point out just a few of the quality attributes you will possess with the skill of living your days as an enthusiastic person.

When we daydream about our future, we see ourselves as enthusiastic. We see ourselves happy and excited: a person of influence and character.

The process starts with the conscious decision on your part to live every day in a state of enthusiasm. Start immediately, not sometime in the future. Today is the day.

I often hear, "I'm going through something right now; I will start when this passes." The truth is, you have been telling yourself that story for years; the challenge is just wearing different clothes. Today is the day. Make a decision: live under *the power of enthusiasm* and make it an amazing one.

Helpful Exercise

Living every day in a constant state of enthusiasm will go a long way in our quest for a *Success Explosion*. The question is, how do we carry on an enthusiastic attitude mentally? As we travel through our days, they can be sometimes get a little hectic.

The answer is to create a list of a couple items in our life that we would consider "awesome." Then reflect on them all day long.

List three things that you love in your life, or something that's on the horizon and will soon be a part of it.

Awesome Item #1

_____

Awesome Item #2

_____

Awesome Item #3

_____

Every day has a theme: the thing you are reflecting on that particular day. Make sure that every day you are considering these items. When something off the list takes your attention, return to the awesome list once it's finished.

"Enthusiasm moves the world."

Arthur Balfour

Ten

An Optimistic Outlook

Optimism is a vital characteristic for a person to possess. It's also one of those attributes that everyone says they have, when in fact most are not even close to the levels of optimism required. I have repeatedly throughout this book used the phrase "a conscious choice," and once more that principle applies here.

I can't underscore the importance of this concept enough: to consciously make a decision to be an optimistic individual. To decide that we will be glass-half-full people, unlike the masses that seem content to languish through life with glasses half-empty.

When we live our life as an optimistic person, we possess the drive to carry on. I know that this doesn't sound like much, but it is. Life has a way of resembling a contact sport: the knocks just keep on coming.

Considering that most people live their lives a long way from a position of optimism, those knocks can be crippling blows. I'm not in any way suggesting that living in a constant state of optimism makes you immune to life's challenges; it certainly does not. Instead, I am referring to how well an individual handles the ebbs in the ebb and flow of life.

No one experiences a constant flow; no one is void of ebb. However, the more optimistic you are, the better prepared you will be for the ebbs. When those ebbs come, an optimistic mindset will shorten their duration.

Conversely, this also means that a non-optimistic mindset would in turn lengthen that undesired ebb. Most people do not have the required optimism, and thus allow the ebb to have a much larger impact than is really necessary. It can get to the point that moving forward can become challenging.

We are all looking to reduce stress in our lives; in fact, there are hundreds of books on that exact topic. If we know that *an optimistic outlook* shortens the duration of life's challenges, and we also know that it's life's challenges that cause stress, we can do ourselves a big favour by not spending so much time there.

When challenges come our way, they are real; I'm not pretending that they're not. We will all experience the ebb and flow of life; no one is exempt. If our next ebb is something life-changing—a ten on a scale of one to ten—I'm not suggesting that you should downplay or neglect it. Life may have dealt us a hand that we would prefer not to play, but still we must.

An optimistic outlook will not in any way negate the situation; however, it could definitely alter our approach when it comes to handling it.

If the hand we were dealt in this game of life is a six on a scale from one to ten, an optimistic attitude will allow you to keep this challenge at a six. Most people deal with the tens at a ten and elevate the sixes to tens. We should deal with our challenges at the same face value they have been dealt to us: sixes should remain sixes, threes should be threes.

The pessimistic mindset tends to dwell where an optimistic mindset looks for solutions. A solution found quickly dispenses of the challenge, in turn eliminating any unnecessary stress and quickly moving you back to the positive side of life, the flow.

Let's take a look at some of the other benefits of purposefully living your life in a constant state of optimism.

Discover New Opportunities

It's a shame how many opportunities can go undiscovered due to the unnecessary time spent dwelling on the ebbs. It's really difficult to say what percentage of your life should be lived in the flow versus the ebb; I suppose it would depend on a lot on your circumstances.

However, I would be comfortable to suggest that the vast majority should be experienced on the positive side. The ebb and flow of life certainly is not a fifty-fifty proposition; your positive experiences should far outweigh those occupying the negative side. I would say that for me, personally, the flow of life is probably between ninety and ninety-five percent, and the negative ebbs are only five to ten percent.

I don't want you to think that I'm just naturally good at all the principles in this book; there are many that I'm still working on. Take this chapter, for example. For some people, a positive mindset comes naturally; however, for most, myself included, it's a learned trait.

Setbacks are a form of change, and just like all change, they come with opportunity; there are definitely some personal growth moments that will take place. However, I'm sure you would agree that it's way more fun to spend our days on the positive side of the ledger.

Although we cannot eliminate from our life those situations that we would prefer not to experience, we can still shift the scale.

Take a moment to honestly estimate how much time you spend on the positive side of the equation. You may have to admit that perhaps, when a challenge visits, you may have inadvertently invested too much time dwelling on it instead of learning from the experience and looking for a solution. That solution is your vehicle back to the positive side of your life.

Life has many opportunities for us at every level of our being; if we accidently spend too much of our valuable time obsessing over the things that are not quite going our way, we miss out on the plethora of discoveries that are available to us. So let's avoid it, as that would be a shame!

Keeps Things in Perspective

Possessing *an optimistic outlook* allows a person the luxury of keeping life's ups and downs at an even keel. Although life has that natural ebb and flow, how we manage and process those day-to-day visitors is very important.

If today's visitor happens to be occupying the positive side of the ledger, it's important that we dial that back (just a bit!) and not let our emotions get too caught up in this item that went our way.

On the other hand, if our visitor happens to be on the negative side of the equation, it's equally important that we don't allow ourselves to be drawn too low.

An optimistic person, whether through natural aptitude or learned skill, is in a position to *keep things in perspective*: not getting too high with the wins or diving too deep with the losses.

Wins and losses are going to happen; that's a guarantee. Life is going to be a lot less stressful for the person that manages those ups and downs with a more level-headed approach. Life is not designed to resemble one big roller coaster ride, with exhilarating ups and crashing lows.

Balance and Fulfillment

Of all the motivational or self-help books written, balance might be the most common topic. It seems that everyone is looking for balance: it can be elusive. I have personally heard speakers suggest that pursuing balance is a futile effort: that it's unachievable, and not worth pursuing.

For the record, I don't agree: not only is balance attainable, it's easier than you think.

First, we need to establish that balance and fulfillment are a feeling; a state of mind. When we consider our lives "balanced," we are living in a state of contentment. We have fulfilled all the aspects of our lives, and they appear to be in order. We enjoy our work, family life is going well, we are comfortable with our spiritual position, and everyone is healthy.

I agree that physically living in perfect balance, where every category of your life is going well all the time, would be hard to attain. However, there is a difference between physically having the perfect balance and achieving mental fulfillment and balance.

If everything had to be "right" all the time in order to live in a state of balance, then of course we would all be out of balance most of the time.

However, if we can live under the assumption that balance and fulfillment are a state of mind, we can strive toward achieving it. We consciously won't get too high on the highs and too low on the lows; we would find a way to *keep things in perspective*. In that scenario, it would be much easier to attain a feeling of calm balance, even though there may currently be challenges in certain aspects of our lives.

Achieving physical balance—i.e. being in the position that all the aspects of your life are working properly all the time—would be beyond difficult, I agree. However, the optimistic person realizes that balance is a state of mind. So even though several aspects may be lacking, they can be pulled along by the others that are working.

Living your days in a constant state of balance, and thus carrying a state of contentment along with you, simply requires you to hedge your emotions. Be aware of the natural ebb and flow of life, and do not let your emotions get carried away with the ups and downs. Even though several challenges may be present, your mind will remain calm and collected: in other words, in balance.

Unfortunately, every coin has two sides: therefore, a person who cannot manage to find a way to take the edge off life's highs and lows will never experience a feeling

144

of balance. Even when they are temporarily experiencing a positive effect in every aspect of their lives, the sense of balance will be absent. It's really a matter of a mental state versus a physical situation.

Promotes Gratitude

The individual living their days in a constant state of optimism tends to automatically adopt a *state of gratitude*. On the other hand, the opposite is also true; the individual who chooses to exist as a pessimistic person tends to live without it. This can harbour a number of negative attributes, including being disloyal, critical, and judgemental—just to name a few.

When we are old and reflect back on our lives, it would be nice if we could do so with satisfaction. Living in a state of optimism goes a long way to making that the case.

I think we need to carefully examine how we process our experiences and how much mental weight we attach to them. One thing is for certain: none of us are getting out of this life alive. We would be wise to not attach so much emotion to life's natural ebb and flow.

At the end of the day, the optimistic individual tends to live in a *state of gratitude*, thankful in every way for the things they have. They may be working diligently on many levels to achieve more, but that in no way makes them less grateful for what they have.

The ungrateful person spends their time comparing themselves to others, and unfortunately cannot find a way to be sincerely happy for another's success. You have a choice. I would suggest you to consciously be a person *living in a state of gratitude*; life's much better that way.

Builds Resilience

Resilience is an interestingly sought-after attribute; when you are truly resilient, life's ups and downs seem to roll right off you.

Obviously, everyone would love to add this attribute to their list. We know for a fact that challenges will come our way. Thus, I'm sure I'm not the only one in need of some resilience from time to time; situations that try our resolve present themselves on a regular basis.

It's a fact that optimistic people are considerably more resilient than those that have not yet acquired this outlook. Optimistic people *get over things quickly,* mostly because they don't make mountains out of molehills. Situations are not escalated. If problems are received at a ten, they are processed at a ten; if they are received at a five, they are processed at a five.

It goes without saying that non-optimistic people handle all challenges at a ten, regardless of the level the challenge introduced itself. This makes it harder to resist those situations. Life is short: let's consciously choose to be resilient, optimistic people, and avoid the unnecessary emotion and drama.

Life has enough real issues without us fabricating worse scenarios that don't really exist. In life, it is best to be both optimistic and resilient.

Reduces Worry

Nothing good comes from worry. Most traits come with a pros and a cons list; not worry. With worry, everything is a con. If we could eliminate worry from our lives, we could save ourselves a lot of personal anguish.

Unfortunately, worry transcends the mental side of life and encroaches on the physical. It's common knowledge that constant worry will bring with it a host of ailments. It's bad enough that constant worry hinders our forward mental progress; however, when worry makes the jump to affecting our body in a negative way, it is much more dramatic. At that point, we have brought unnecessary physical hardship upon ourselves.

As we travel through life, sickness will visit many people. All families, at some point, will deal with such a challenge. Sometimes it is those that made all the healthy choices that are afflicted—the random lot in life.

Therefore, we would be wise to eliminate any additional risk of being struck with an illness. If worry can cause a negative physical condition, we might as well do our best to eliminate this one from our risk group.

I read the other day that most of what we worry about

never happens. In other words, the majority of what we worry about never comes to pass. So why dwell?

Optimistic people worry less; they are, by their very nature, glass-half-full people. When we are viewing the glass half-full, we are automatically observing possibilities: what could be.

On the other hand, viewing the glass as half-empty is considering potential problems or what is lacking; viewing the glass half-empty is where the worry resides.

By seeing the potential in everything around us, we are distancing ourselves from the mistake of focussing on worry. For example, say you are looking at a glass on your left, and it is half-empty. When you turn to your right, there is another glass, this time half-full.

Whichever direction you are looking in, you do not see what occupies the other space. Therefore, you can eliminate worry by simply not looking in that direction.

Optimistic people don't gaze in the direction of worry, or get involved with any of the other negative characteristics that hang out in the glass-half-empty zone. Be optimistic, and *reduce your worry*.

In a Nutshell

Optimism is an amazing characteristic to possess, and an ideal way to experience life. Being an optimistic person is the gateway to fulfilling your dreams: everything you want starts with *an optimistic outlook*.

To the optimistic person, the doors of opportunity are always open. To some, it may appear as though they are catching all the breaks, or are genuinely lucky. When in fact, the doors of opportunity are propped wide open due to their unwavering, optimistic attitude.

It is optimistic people who experience stress-free, balanced lives. For them, there are no challenges that the worrying brain has manufactured and put in their way.

It's those with *an optimistic outlook* that enjoy the benefits of *living in a state of gratitude,* all items that reside in the glass-half-full spectrum.

You have a choice: to either be an optimistic person, or to spend your days being negative. Choose optimism!

Helpful Exercise

These exercises might be familiar, which is a good point: they certainly are. However, the more ways you can think correctly, the better. Optimistic people are excited about their lives: both what they currently have and those things that are still in their path.

List a couple of items that you are currently excited about, and a few items you are still tracking down.

Amazing Item Currently in My Life #1:

_____

Amazing Item Currently in My Life #2:

_____

Amazing Item I'm Tracking Down #1:

_____

Amazing Item I'm Tracking Down #2:

_____

When we have a couple of items in our lives that we are really excited about, and a few more coming down the pipeline, it's really easy to be optimistic. We just need to keep those things as our primary focus each and every day.

"In life, you have a choice: to be either optimistic or pessimistic. Choose optimism."

Anonymous

Final Thoughts
Living With Passion

We all have a desire to live our days in a constant state of passion; unfortunately for most, this worthwhile goal will inevitably go unrealized. Most seek passion first, not realizing that passion is a collection of positive attributes.

There is a reason that the topic of passion occupies the final thoughts rather than one of the chapters. Passion is a result of mastering chapters one through ten. Therefore, it is vital that we do our utmost to integrate the following concepts into our lives:

Get Over Things Quickly

Live in a State of Gratitude

Set Worthwhile Goals

Never Give Up

The Blessing of Contribution

Positive Expectation

Embrace Change

A Determined Spirit

The Power of Enthusiasm

An Optimistic Outlook

Any person adhering to the above attributes will become a passionate person, which also means that being void of these characteristics would make passion virtually impossible.

If you were to spend a rainy afternoon completing a jigsaw puzzle, you would not consider the puzzle complete until all the pieces were in place. This is the exact same thing. In your quest to have a *Success Explosion,* all of these pieces will need to be aligned and in place in your life. The more you implement the principles of this book, the more passionate you will automatically become.

All of these characteristics are considered positive attributes, and are necessary to be considered a person of character. Good character is a mandatory quality to be a person of passion. If you are void of a number of these attributes, then you are only pretending at having passion; it is only those that purposefully train themselves to acquire the necessary attributes who will attain true passion.

Being a truly passionate person does not necessarily mean that you have it all together; it just means that you know what "all together" looks like. You certainly don't have to be all the way down the path; you just need to know where the path is.

Living in a state of passion is an exciting way to live, and should be sought out by all individuals. Adhering to the principles of this book will automatically result in the daily passion that you desire.

I trust that you have found this information helpful, and I truly hope that I have, in some small way, assisted you in achieving a *Success Explosion* in every aspect of your life.

GOD BLESS!

Helpful Exercise

Obviously, living our days as a passionate person would be a great scenario for any of us. We probably have some items in our lives that we could purposefully increase our passion toward. Perhaps a relationship, or some other goal in one of the aspects of our lives. If we were to become more passionate about that aspect, our odds of achieving that result would increase.

List three areas of your life that you could increase your passion for:

I need to increase my passion in the following area #1:

_____

_____

I need to increase my passion in the following area #2:

_____

_____

I need to increase my passion in the following area #3:

_____

_____

Increasing your passion in these areas will assist you in your overall quest for a life driven toward a *Success Explosion*.

"You can't do anything about the length of your life. But you can do something about its width and depth."

Evan Esar

Notes